The Rosary

Your Weapon for Spiritual Warfare

JOHNNETTE S. BENKOVIC

and

THOMAS K. SULLIVAN

servant

AN IMPRINT OF
FRANCISCAN MEDIA
Cincinnati, Ohio

Cover design by Michael Frazier

LIBRARY OF CONGRESS CATALOGING-IN-PUBLICATION DATA

Names: Benkovic, Johnnette S., author. | Sullivan, Thomas K., author.

Title: The rosary : your weapon for spiritual warfare / Johnnette S. Benkovic and Thomas K. Sullivan.

Description: Cincinnati, Ohio : Servant, 2017. | Includes bibliographical references.

Identifiers: LCCN 2016059145 | ISBN 9781632530004 (paperback)

Subjects: LCSH: Rosary. | BISAC: RELIGION / Christian Life / Prayer. | RELIGION / Christian Life / Spiritual Warfare. | RELIGION / Christianity / Catholic.

Classification: LCC BX2163 .B38 2017 | DDC 242/.74—dc23

LC record available at https://lccn.loc.gov/2016059145

ISBN 978-1-63253-000-4

Published by Servant, an imprint of
Franciscan Media
28 W. Liberty St.
Cincinnati, OH 45202
www.FranciscanMedia.org

Printed in the United States of America.
Printed on acid-free paper.
17 18 19 20 21   5 4 3 2 1

With gratitude, I dedicate this book to my grandmother, Julia E. Simon, whose faithful prayer of the Rosary became a lifeline of hope and healing for me and whose example inspired me to hold on to the hand of Mary in the most difficult moment of my life. May Gram Simon be at peace in the Lord.

Additionally, I dedicate this book to my daughters and their families. You bring me such joy! Continue to keep these holy beads in your hands, asking Our Blessed Lady to reveal to you ever more deeply the mysteries of her Son's life, for they will surely lead you to the fullness of life in Him, Our Lord Jesus Christ.

—Johnnette S. Benkovic

I dedicate this book to my beautiful Filipina wife (my *asawa*), Carolina Dejanio Sullivan. For over thirty-five years, she has been the wind beneath my wings and the love that fills my heart. She is my spiritual "little sniper," who has always had my back with her constant prayer support, and a true warrior princess of God Most High.

To my children—Jeffrey, Tommy, Maria, Michael, Joshua, and Gabriel—each of whom sets my fatherly heart ablaze with love in his or her own unique way. You are the arrows in my quiver on the battlefield of life. May you always keep The Warrior's Rosary close to your hearts as you soldier through life serving Our Lord and Our Lady in the kingdom family of God.

—Thomas K. Sullivan

Contents

Pope John Paul II, in his apostolic letter *Rosarium Virginis Mariae*, tells us that the Rosary "marks the rhythm of human life" (*RVM*, 2). Through the years, I have come to discover the truth of this beautiful statement. This sacred prayer and its holy beads have been my comfort, my joy, and a mighty weapon for spiritual warfare.

I cannot recollect the exact moment I first saw a Rosary, but I am certain the beads must have been in my grandmother's hands. Gram Simon's hands were rarely without her Rosary beads, unless she was cooking a dinner, baking a pie, dusting the house, doing the laundry, or hugging one of us kids. I remember family trips with Gram and Gramp and my girl cousins. We liked riding in their car, because it was spacious and had air conditioning, even back in 1959. Every trip began with the Rosary. Gram would lead, and Gramp would chime in with part two of the prayers.

I have to honestly tell you that I couldn't wait until the Rosary was over so we girls could get to talking about really important things, like what we would do when we got to

Geneva-on-the-Lake, a beach town on Lake Erie in Ohio. Little did I know that, even then, Gram's prayers were storing up graces for me that would affect my future. Many years later, I would learn that Gram prayed a Rosary a day for each one of her thirteen grandchildren. That's thirteen Rosaries a day, and one of them always had my name on it.

The years passed, and off I went to university. Campus life was rife with dissent in those days. The sexual revolution and all that attended it were in full swing. I would like to say I remained unscathed by it all, but that would be untrue. Putting my Catholic upbringing and education on the back burner, I became involved in the hedonistic lifestyle of the time. But Gram was praying away, and occasionally I received a note from her telling me so.

Though I made a dramatic change before my senior year began, damage had been done, and it would take me ten years to come back to the faith. When I did, I realized it was Gram Simon's Rosaries that tilled the hardened soil of my heart so that the seed of truth could be planted, grow deep roots, and produce the fruit of conversion. Gram waged a battle for my soul, and her weapon of choice was the prayer of the Rosary.

The Rosary became an important part of my devotional practice, but the joy and beauty of it remained elusive. There were times when the light of grace broke through, and I could see that the Rosary was far more than the rote recitation of formula prayers. I wanted to go deeper, and yet, for the most part, the Rosary remained a rather long, monotonous affair, during which I had to fight distraction, boredom, and sleep. Indeed, the prayer of the Rosary was a battlefield. (See the *Catechism of the Catholic Church*, [*CCC*] 2725–2728, for more on the battle of prayer.)

Things changed the morning of March 20, 2004, when two Florida state highway patrolmen came to the door of our home to tell us that our son, Simon, had been killed in a vehicular accident at 1:01 A.M. In this moment of deepest travail, I turned to our Blessed Mother, seeking her maternal beatitude to make this time a sacrifice of praise to the Father, Son, and Holy Spirit. In the exceedingly rough days and weeks that followed, I clung to my Rosary as if the air I breathed depended upon it. Spiritually speaking, it did.

During those weeks, it was as if Mary was walking me through the mysteries of her Son's life, sharing with me the intimacies of grace each one contained, that I might find the strength and confidence to go on. Sometimes these came by heavenly light; other times I was not even aware of the profound graces being imparted. But the effects were clear. Mary took my weakness and gave me her strength; she took my fear and gave me her trust; she took my insecurity and gave me her confidence. And it all came by way of the Rosary.

Since Simon's death, the power of the Rosary and its efficacy as *the* weapon of spiritual warfare has been impressed upon me ever more deeply. It is my firm conviction that St. Dominic's words are true: "*One day, through the Rosary and the Scapular, Our Lady will save the world.*"[1] "In the end," Mary told the children at Fatima, Portugal, in 1917, "My Immaculate Heart will triumph."[2] And indeed, it will.

By the divine pleasure of the Father, Mary invites us to enter into the mysteries of faith presented to us through the holy Rosary and to receive the graces they offer. As we are transformed more and more by their power and light, we can come to "the stature of the fullness of Christ" (Ephesians 4:13). And we can battle against the powers of darkness to bring this our day and time into the victory of the cross. It is to this end that we have written this book. May it achieve what God intends.

Johnnette S. Benkovic

July 16, 2016

Feast of Our Lady of Mount Carmel

Chapter One

The Rosary

A WEAPON FOR ALL TIME

Some people are so foolish that they think they
can go through life without the help of the Blessed
Mother. Love the Madonna and pray the Rosary,
for her Rosary is the weapon against the evils of the
world today. All graces given by God pass through
the Blessed Mother.[1]

—St. Padre Pio

Today we face unprecedented challenges on every
front. The evils of "this present darkness" weigh heavy
against us. Perhaps this is what makes the advice of St. Padre
Pio, a holy man from our own age, so valuable and insightful.
He reminds us of the Rosary's power against the devil and
his minions, and he reminds us of the efficacy of the Blessed
Virgin's mediation for us through it. Pope Pius XII's words,

too, seem right and fitting: "We put great confidence in the Holy Rosary for the healing of evils which afflict our times."[2]

What makes this prayer so powerful and effective? One indication may be found in its earliest reference. It seems it was born out of the strife, sacrifice, and persecution of the early Church martyrs. The term *Rosary* comes from the Latin *Rosarium*, which means "crown of roses" or "garland of roses."

As young virgins prepared to walk into the arena of the Coliseum to face the beasts that would tear them asunder, they made ready to meet Jesus Christ, King of Kings, for whom they were offering their lives. They fittingly adorned themselves in festive garments, with crowns of roses for their heads. Thus bedecked, they joined their Savior in His Passion. At night, the faithful would gather up the martyrs' crowns and say their prayers on them, one prayer for each rose.[3] Their prayer was a journey, perhaps, into the mystery of what they had witnessed.[4]

Using a device to count prayers was common in the Church. In the fourth century, the Desert Fathers kept track of their devotions on prayer cords. In the fifth century, St. Brigid of Ireland strung pieces of stone and wood together to form a little wreath, and upon these pieces, she would pray the Our Father, the Hail Mary, and the Creed.[5]

During this same time, it became the custom of Christians in both East and West to divide the psalter into three groups of fifty psalms each and pray or chant them in public. The custom was adapted for those who were uneducated or poor, or who toiled in the fields far away from the churches. These substituted fifty repetitions of the Angelic salutation (Ave Maria) for the fifty psalms.[6] These *Aves* were recited along with verses from the Gospel relating to the joys of Mary, such as the Annunciation, Nativity, Resurrection, Ascension, and Assumption.

This style of prayer became known as a *Rosarium.* According to writings by the Venerable Bede, churches in England and France were making prayer beads available to the faithful by the eighth century.[7]

The first clear historical reference we have to the Rosary as we know it today dates back to the thirteenth century, from the life of St. Dominic, founder of the Order of Preachers, or Dominicans. According to tradition, Dominic devised the Rosary after Our Lady appeared to him and told him to pray in this manner as an antidote for heresy and sin. He obeyed, and he preached the Rosary with great success in France during the time of the Albigensian heresy.

One of the most famous miracles of the Rosary was performed at the hands of St. Dominic. He expelled thousands of demons from a possessed man in front of a crowd of twelve thousand, after putting a Rosary around the man's neck.[8]

In spite of this and many other spectacular miracles, the Rosary fell into disuse until two centuries later, when a Dominican theologian named Blessed Alain de la Roche (d. 1475) made it his life's mission to restore the devotion. He is credited with establishing Rosary confraternities to promote the Rosary and developing what is known as the "Dominican Rosary." This Rosary included three groups of mysteries related to the Incarnation, the Passion, and the Resurrection of Christ. This became the most popular form of the Rosary.

The beads underwent many changes over time with special devotions, local customs, and even the latest fashions impacting the style in use. For instance, a short form of the Rosary, containing only ten beads and known as a "tenner" (also called a "decade Rosary"), was a favorite among men.[9] Women liked the longer version, and they often adorned their Rosaries with gems, pearls, miniature figurines, and even scented fruits and flowers.

Rosaries have been made of everything from pure gold to painted apricot pits. Filigree Rosaries were popular in the eighteenth century, and chain-stitched Rosaries were the rage during the nineteenth. Also during this time, the three beads for the theological virtues of faith, hope, and charity were added to the beginning of the Rosary.

No matter the enhancements, adornments, and forms that have graced this sacramental over the years, we cannot lose sight of the fact that the Rosary is first and foremost a powerful spiritual weapon. It has been credited with some of the greatest triumphs in history. Here are just a few of them!

THE BATTLE OF LEPANTO, 1571

The Rosary grew in popularity and became the spiritual weapon of choice in the 1500s. At this time, Moslem Turks were ravaging Eastern Europe. In 1571, when it seemed as though the whole continent would fall under their control, Pope St. Pius V stepped into action. Perceiving the great threat posed by the forward advancement of the Ottoman Empire, he formed the Holy League, an alliance of most of the Catholic maritime forces of the Mediterranean. He then asked all of the faithful to say the Rosary and beg for Mary's intercession for victory over the Turks.

The famous battle, known as the Battle of Lepanto, took place October 7, 1571. It is recognized by historians as the most important naval contest in human history. Pope Pius V would commemorate the date by making it a feast day of the Church, in honor of the one whose intercession made the victory possible.

The pope chose Don Juan of Austria to be the general of the League. He was the illegitimate son of the late Holy Roman Emperor Charles V and the half-brother of Philip II, King of Spain. Though only twenty-four, Don Juan was a capable leader. He was a great swordsman and horseman, and he had distinguished himself in battle against the Barbary corsairs in the Morisco rebellion of Spain.[10] He was handsome, popular with the ladies of the court, and deeply devoted to the Blessed Virgin Mary. He was known to use his sword valiantly and swiftly when needed but to prudently and justly resist when not.

Brandon Rogers, commenting on G.K. Chesterton's epic poem *Lepanto*, says that Pope Pius V had both a physical and spiritual plan of attack. The Holy Father was counting on the Turkish fleet to accept the challenge of the Holy League. He told Don Juan, "I take it for certain that the Turks, swollen by their victories, will wish to take on our fleet, and God—I have the presentiment—will give us the victory."[11]

The pontiff knew this was a holy war with high stakes. Islam's goal was to take Europe and most specially to conquer Rome. For this war, then, the pope knew he would need both "the prayers of priests of pure life" and holy warriors. God granted him both.

To Don Juan, the pope's words could not have been clearer. He took command of his fleet with a series of orders and an invitation: No women could be aboard the fleet, blasphemy would be punishable by death, and the crew was welcome to join him in a three-day fast. On the decks of the Holy League galleys, priests of various religious orders offered Mass and heard confessions.

Many of the oarsmen were criminals. Promising them their freedom in exchange for fighting bravely, Don Juan released them from their fetters, armed them, and then gave each the most powerful weapon of all—a Rosary. He told the men that the battle they faced was as much spiritual as it was physical.

The night before engagement, the men of the Holy League knelt on the galley decks and prayed the Rosary. They were joined up and down the Italian peninsula, as well as throughout Europe, by the faithful, who had filled the churches at the request of Pius V. These faithful, too, plied their beads with fervent petition for a victorious outcome. Our Lady was listening.

At predawn on the morning of October 7, 1571, the Holy Sacrifice of the Mass was celebrated on the decks of the Holy

League's galleys. Pope Pius V had directed the priests to grant general absolution to each man who would serve and die that day.

From the beginning, the odds seemed to be against the forces of Don Juan. Fog, mist, and strong headwinds made for a difficult journey through the choppy sea. The fleet worked its way south into the Gulf of Patras. As they rounded into its narrows, they saw in the distance the enormous war galleys of the Ottoman Empire, coming from the east in full battle array. Their formation was that of a giant crescent, the symbol of Islam.

As the Holy League struggled to make its approach, the men could see the battle pennant of Muezzinzade Ali Pasha, the Muslim commander, flying from the mast of his ship. Green and gold, it was covered with verses from the Qur'an and embroidered with the name "Allah" nine hundred times in gold calligraphy. It was the very banner the prophet Mohammed had taken into battle. This symbol, sacred to the Muslims, had never been captured.

Don Juan observed the situation and decided to engage. He ordered the Holy League's battle pennant, previously blessed by the Holy Father, to be run up the mast of the *Real*, his command ship. The banner unfurled to reveal the crucified Christ. Priests moved through the galleys blessing the men with raised crucifixes and hearing last-minute confessions. The men, Rosaries in hand, implored the help of the Blessed Virgin.

The fleet fell into a cruciform battle position. The cross and the crescent were about to engage.

Don Juan reminded the men of their mission: They had come to defend Christianity. "Do your duty," he exhorted them, "and you will secure a glorious immortality."[12] With the winds buffeting him, he raised his eyes to heaven and begged God to bless his people with victory. Observing his example, the officers and men on every vessel followed suit.

And then the miraculous happened. Our Lady intervened! The headwinds did an about-face and began to blow directly against the Muslim fleet! Holy League sails were raised. Ottoman sails were dropped. Then, propelled as if by heaven's breath, the Holy League closed in on its adversary.

It was midday when the fleets engaged. They fought for five long hours. In the end, the Turks' bows and arrows were no match against the guns of the Holy League. Key to the win was the head-on collision of the two flagships. Both generals broke with the convention of galley warfare that commanders' ships would not engage. The Holy League's *Real*, commanded by Don Juan, and the Turks' *Sultana*, commanded by Ali Pasha, collided with tremendous force, and a deadly duel commenced. It was a fight to the finish, with much bloodshed.[13]

Don Juan was wounded, but Ali Pasha mortally so. A musket ball to the forehead felled him. One of Don Juan's men severed Pasha's head and carried it to the quarterdeck of the *Real* as a symbol of victory. The men of the *Sultana* capitulated when they saw their leader's grisly end. The prophet's sacred banner came down, and the papal banner was raised to the Christians' cheers and cries of "Victory."

Interestingly, on the day of the battle, Pope Pius V was in a meeting with his cardinals. In the midst of their deliberations, he paused and walked to the window. As he gazed at the sky, a vision from Our Lady showed him the victory of the Holy League. He turned to his cardinals, saying, "Let us set aside business and fall on our knees in thanksgiving to God, for he has given our fleet a great victory."[14]

In thanksgiving, the pope established the Feast of Our Lady of Victory to forever memorialize the great triumph wrought by the powerful intercession of the Mother of God. In time, October 7 became known as the Feast of Our Lady of the Rosary.

OUR LADY OF FATIMA, 1917

In 1917, the powerful prayer of the Rosary took on another urgent moment. The "Great War," which came to be known as World War I, was raging. With over seventy million military personnel engaged, it was to become one of the largest wars in history. At this point, the Mother of God appeared to three shepherd children in Fatima, Portugal, with a warning and a request that was meant to save the world.

For six consecutive months, from May 13 to October 13, the Blessed Mother appeared to Lucia dos Santos, age nine, and her cousins, Francisco and Jacinta Marto, ages eight and six. The children tended sheep in the Cova da Iria, a portion of land owned by Antonio dos Santos, Lucia's father. On May 13, something like lightning flashed in the blue sky and frightened them. The children ran for cover. Another flash, very close, and they ran again. When they stopped, there on top of a small evergreen tree was a large ball of light engulfing a beautiful woman, "a Lady of all white, more brilliant than the sun dispensing light."

The beautiful woman told the children not to be afraid. Lucia asked her where she had come from and what she wanted. The lovely lady said she was from heaven, and she wanted them to return at the same time on the thirteenth day for the following five months. At the last visit, she would identify herself and tell the children what she wanted.

Lucia then asked if she and her cousins would go to heaven. The woman said yes but advised that Francisco would need to pray many Rosaries first.

The lady asked the children if they were willing to offer themselves to God and to bear the sufferings He would send. He desired that they offer their sufferings as an act of reparation for the sins by which He was offended and as an act of supplication for the conversion of sinners.

Lucia thought about another heavenly being who had visited her and her cousins. An angel who identified himself as the "Angel of Peace" had appeared to them three times—in the spring, summer, and autumn of 1916. He gave them Holy Communion and exhorted them to pray and make sacrifices. It seemed as if the Angel of Peace had prepared the children for their response to the Lady's question. Lucia answered for all three of them, "Yes."

"Then you are going to have much to suffer, but the grace of God will be your comfort," the Lady replied.

At that moment, the children were infused with a heavenly light. They felt the presence of God and offered prayers of adoration. When they were finished, the Lady said, "Say the Rosary, to obtain peace for the world and the end of the war." With that, the beautiful woman rose from the bush and glided away into the sky. That was Sunday, May 13, 1917.

When the day arrived for the second apparition, several people accompanied the children to the Cova. Our Blessed Lady asked the children to recite five decades of the Rosary each day and told them they were to learn to read. She told Lucia she would live a long life, but her cousins would go to heaven soon. When Lucia expressed her sorrow at this, Our Lady said that her Immaculate Heart would be her refuge.

Then Our Lady extended her hands, and great shafts of light poured upon the children. All three of them saw a vision of the Immaculate Heart and were filled with indescribable joy and peace.

On July 13, the date of the third apparition, nearly three thousand people gathered at the Cova da Iria. When the Blessed Mother appeared to the children, she reminded them to pray the Rosary for peace. And then something remarkable occurred. Shafts of light flowed from Our Lady's hands through the children to the earth below them. The ground seemed to roll back, and the three visionaries stared into the pit of hell. Years later, Lucia wrote of what they saw: "A sea of fire; and plunged in this fire the demons and the souls, as if they were red-hot coals."

Our Lady explained to the children:

You have seen hell where the souls of poor sinners go. To save them, God wishes to establish in the world devotion to my Immaculate Heart. If what I say to you is done, many souls will be saved and there will be peace. The war [World War I] is going to end: but if people do not cease offending God, a worse one will break out during the Pontificate of Pius XI. When you see a night illumined by an unknown light, know that this is the great sign given you by God that he is about to punish the world for its crimes, by means of war, famine, and persecutions of the Church and of the Holy Father. To prevent this, I shall come to ask for the consecration of Russia to my Immaculate Heart and the Communion of reparation on the First Saturdays. If my requests are heeded, Russia will be converted, and there will be peace; if not, she will spread her errors throughout the world, causing wars and persecutions of the Church. The good will be martyred; the Holy Father will have much to suffer; various nations will be annihilated. In the end, my Immaculate Heart will triumph. The Holy Father will consecrate Russia to me, and she shall be converted, and a period of peace will be granted to the world.[15]

This prophetic word was astonishing for a number of reasons. First of all, the Blessed Mother accurately predicted the elevation of Pope Pius XI, who would not become pontiff until 1922. Secondly, at the time of this apparition, the Russian Revolution had not occurred. The Bolsheviks would take over the following October, and they would legalize abortion without restriction, institute no-fault divorce, and strive to squelch belief in God.[16]

Thirdly, as Our Lady predicted, communism subsequently spread its errors and atheistic philosophy all over the world. Fourthly, World War II followed the first Great War during the pontificate of Pope Pius XI and into that of Pope Pius XII. That war introduced the atom bomb and caused even more destruction than World War I.

The month following the third apparition was particularly difficult for the visionaries. The children were besieged daily by visitors and curiosity seekers. In addition, an anticlerical republic had come into power in Portugal, and the local authorities were keen on putting an end to the Fatima piety. Things came to a head when the government administrator carted the children away under false pretenses on August 13, the day scheduled for the fourth apparition. The children were threatened with death unless they revealed the secrets Our Lady had entrusted to them. When Francisco said it didn't matter if they were killed since they would go straight to heaven, the children were released.

Thousands of people greeted the children at the Cova on September 13. The apparition was short in duration, but the Blessed Mother promised that the children would see the Lord, Our Lady of Sorrows, Our Lady of Mount Carmel, and St. Joseph with the Child Jesus at the next apparition. More than seventy thousand people gathered on October 13. Their parents feared the children would be killed if no miracle took place.

It was a rainy and windy day. Umbrellas dotted the landscape as the children knelt to pray. For a reason she does not know, Lucia encouraged the crowd to close their umbrellas.

When the Blessed Mother appeared, Lucia asked her one last time, "What do you want of me?" Our Lady responded, "I want to tell you to have them build a chapel here in my honor. I am the Lady of the Rosary. Let them continue to say the Rosary every day. The war is going to end, and the soldiers will soon return to their homes."

Lucia told Our Lady that many who had come were seeking healing. The Blessed Mother said they first needed to amend their lives so they would no longer offend God. He was already much offended, she told Lucia. These would be Our Lady's last words at Fatima. She opened her hands again, and light shot to the sky.

"Look at the sky!" shouted Lucia. The miracle of the sun had begun. It became a white disc of light that all could gaze upon. While this was happening, the children saw a tableau in the heavens, with one scene after the other depicting the mysteries of the Rosary. They saw the Holy Family with the Christ Child in the arms of St. Joseph, who blessed the crowd three times. Lucia saw Our Lady of Sorrows and then Our Lady of Mount Carmel.

The sun danced in the sky, twirling and whirling, shooting rainbow-colored rays all over the earth. The crowd and the landscape were bathed in green, then violet, then red, as the sun continued its spinning dance. Shouts of praise and worship rose to the heavens as the crowd delighted in the light show they were seeing.

Suddenly, the movement of the sun began to change. It plunged toward the earth, falling ever closer to the people. The panic-stricken crowd dropped to their knees to beg God's mercy. Just as the sun seemed about to touch the earth, it began to recede, eventually assuming its normal position in the sky. To the astonishment of everyone gathered at the Cova, their rain-drenched clothing was dry as was everything about them. Truly, it was a "Miracle of the Sun."

Not long after the apparitions ended, Francisco and Jacinta died, he of bronchial pneumonia on April 4, 1919, and she of pleurisy on February 20, 1920. In June 1921, Lucia entered a school run by the Sisters of St. Dorothy at Porto. She joined that order in 1925, eventually leaving it to become a cloistered Carmelite in Coimbra. She took the name Sr. Mary of the Immaculate Heart.

The Church recognized the apparitions at Fatima as "worthy of belief" in 1930. The Blessed Mother had given three secrets to the children. Two of them were shared immediately, and the third was not to be revealed until 1960 or upon the death of Lucia, whichever came first. Pope John XXIII and Pope Paul VI both read the third secret. Following the attempt on his life on May 13, 1981, Pope John Paul II read it as well. He visited Sr. Lucia the following year, to the day. Afterward, he consecrated the world to the Immaculate Heart of Mary in collegial union with the bishops of the Church. Pope Pius XII had done something similar in 1942.

On June 26, 2000, the Congregation for the Doctrine of the Faith released the third secret in its entirety. The shrine at

Fatima, Portugal, remains one of the most visited apparition sites in the world, with millions of visitors every year.

On February 13, 2005, Sr. Lucia dos Santos died at the age of ninety-seven. One can hope that she is now united with her beloved Jacinta and Francisco, enjoying the company of the beautiful Lady who visited them so many years ago.[17]

Ground Zero, Hiroshima, Japan, 1945

The words of Our Lady of Fatima are prophetic. Just as she predicted, a much greater war came in 1939 and would continue until 1945. And just as she predicted, a gigantic unknown light preceded what would come to be known as the Second World War. As reported by the *New York Times* on January 25, 1938, throughout Europe the night sky was lit with a gigantic aurora that terrified thousands of people. From an airplane, the paper reported, the sky looked like "a shimmering curtain of fire."[18]

During the final stage of World War II, the United States dropped atomic bombs on the Japanese cities of Hiroshima and Nagasaki, killing and wounding tens of thousands of people.[19] In the midst of the unprecedented devastation and destruction, a miracle involving the Rosary occurred at ground zero in Hiroshima.

On the morning of August 6, 1945, at 8:15 A.M., Fr. Hubert Schiffer and seven other Jesuits were sitting down to breakfast at their rectory in Hiroshima. "Suddenly, a terrific explosion filled the air with one bursting thunder stroke," the priest said. "An invisible force lifted me from the chair, hurled me through the air, shook me, battered me, whirled me 'round and 'round like a leaf in a gust of autumn wind."[20]

When his eyes opened, Fr. Schiffer was lying outside on the ground. Dazed, he looked around and saw that, except for the rectory behind him, not a single building on the block was left standing. Although they didn't realize it at the time, Fr. Schiffer and his fellow priests had just survived the blast of the world's first atomic bomb.

Miraculously, the priests suffered only minor injuries, even though the rectory was a mere kilometer from the center of the blast. Many who were close to the epicenter "were simply vaporized by the intensity of the heat."[21] Others were severely burned or were crushed in the collapse of buildings; many would die later of radiation poisoning.[22]

When they comprehended the magnitude of the miracle that had happened, Fr. Schiffer and his fellow priests knew why they were spared. "We believe that we survived because we were living the message of Fatima, and we lived and prayed the Rosary daily in that home," he said.[23]

As if in confirmation, the Franciscan friary in Nagasaki, established by St. Maximilian Kolbe, was also unharmed in an atomic blast that destroyed the city a few days later. The friars were also devoted to the daily recitation of the Rosary. Divine Providence had led St. Maximilian to build the friary in a location that protected it from the full force of the blast.

AUSTRIA'S FIGHT FOR FREEDOM, 1955

Less than a decade later, in the wake of World War II, an army of the Catholic faithful in Austria decided to take on communism. Again, their only weapon was the Rosary.

The battle in Austria began when World War II ended. A massive power struggle erupted in the country between the Allied forces and the communists. The Allies occupied the nation, but the communists held lower Austria, which was rich in oil, agriculture, and industry. Although the communists won only four seats in the freely elected Austrian government, they used their lucrative holdings to bully people and try to topple the government.

While reconstruction following the war was difficult for all Austrians, it was especially so for those living in the Soviet zone. In the three other sectors of Austria, the Allies worked hard to restore equilibrium to the population as well as the economy. However, in the Red sector, the Soviets depleted natural resources, impoverishing the Austrian people. As the Cold War developed, it became apparent that the Soviets had no intention of loosening their grip on lower Austria.

Encouraged by the prayers of holy nuns, on February 2, 1946, a Franciscan priest named Petrus Pavlicek made a special pilgrimage to the famous Marian Shrine at Mariazell. It was the feast day of Our Lady of Lights, and he went to the shrine to beg Our Lady's help for occupied Austria. During his prayers, he heard the voice of Mary within his heart: "Do what I tell you, and there will be peace," she said. She presented again the requests she had made to the three shepherd children at Fatima in 1917.

Fr. Pavlicek responded by founding the Atonement Crusade of the Rosary, a national crusade dedicated to praying for the conversion of sinners, peace in the world, and freedom for Austria. The centerpiece of the crusade was around-the-clock recitation of the Rosary. Fr. Pavlicek asked for a "tithe" of Rosaries: a daily Rosary from at least 10 percent of the Austrian population until the Soviets left the country. Within four years, more than two hundred thousand Austrians made the pledge; by 1955, the number had grown to half a million.

In September 1948, Fr. Pavlicek established the Crusade's Acts of Reparatory Devotion. Held in a Capuchin church in Vienna, these Acts included the Holy Sacrifice of the Mass, sermons, confessions, blessings of the sick and infirm, and recitations of the Rosary. Father referred to these devotions as "assaults of prayer." A "siege" of prayer could last up to five days. "Peace is a gift of God, not the work of politicians," he would remind attendees.

Crusaders organized and staged processions with the statue of Our Lady of Fatima on the thirteenth day of each month. These processions grew so large that Fr. Pavlicek decided to launch an annual procession, to which he invited all of the parishes of Vienna. He chose September 12, the Feast of the Name of Mary, as the date for this annual event in honor of the Blessed Virgin Mary, Queen of Heaven and Earth. This was a meaningful date for Austria and the Viennese in particular. Pope Innocent XI established this feast in 1683 to commemorate the victory of Christian armies over Turkish infidels who had surrounded Vienna. The victory had been won through the intercession of the Blessed Virgin Mary.

Once again, the Austrian people stormed heaven, beseeching Our Lady's maternal beatitude. Among the thousands of people who turned out for the annual procession was Prime Minister Leopold Figl. With Rosary in hand, he marched with his cabinet ministers and his countrymen to seek Mary's assistance. His successor, Julius Raab, participated in the 1953 procession.

Seemingly out of the blue, on the eve of the Annunciation, March 24, 1955, the Russian foreign minister invited an Austrian delegation to Moscow for the first of many conferences about a possible Communist withdrawal from Austria. These talks eventually led to a deal, which was struck on a day that could only have been picked by Our Lady. It was May 13, 1955, the anniversary of the first apparition at Fatima. Two days later, the Austrian State Treaty was signed at the Belvedere Palace in Vienna. Austria was free. This marks the first time in history that militant Marxist forces peacefully left a country in which they held power.[24]

In Vienna, the news was met with great celebration by the faithful who had beseeched heaven. With Rosaries in hand and the statue of Our Lady of Fatima held high, they processed in praise and thanksgiving for the favor received. During a thanksgiving celebration on September 12, 1955, Prime Minister Julius Raab gave credit to Our Lady for the negotiations and ultimate happy outcome: "Today, we, whose hearts are full of faith, cry out to Heaven in joyful prayer. We are free. O Mary, we thank thee!"[25]

Once again, the power of the Rosary, united to a holy *fiat*, brought about a victory that only heaven could have designed.

THE ROSARY CAMPAIGN OF BRAZIL, 1964

Soviet-style Communism was on the march in the early sixties. Brazil was to be a key conquest: Bordered by ten of the other twelve South American countries, Brazil would provide easy access to most of the continent; it was rich in untapped resources; and its capture could lead to the conquest of the West. The grab for power would consist of three consecutive strategies: first chaos, then civil war, and finally, total communist rule.[26]

According to communist calculations, the conquest would come easily. The economy was on the brink of collapse, and with revolution seemingly inevitable, the morale of the populace was low. Radicals were rife under Brazil's president, left-leaning João Goulart. Closet communists serving Moscow's aims had infiltrated government agencies and ministries, and "engineers of chaos"[27] were stirring up unrest among labor union workers and students. Indeed, a "Red Trojan horse" had invaded key administrative posts.[28] The head of the illegal but active Brazilian Communist Party, Luís Carlos Prestes, was already gloating about an imminent takeover.

What President Goulart and his sympathizers didn't count on was a counterrevolution comprised of the normally law-abiding populace. The institutional Church and the strong Catholic faith of the Brazilian people formed a strong force. But especially important among them was the strong anti-communist initiative of Brazil's Catholic women.

A group of concerned anti-Red businessmen and professionals formed the Institute for Economic and Social

Research to investigate what was really taking place within the government. Once they saw, they mobilized. They began by producing dossiers to wake up the tolerant and complacent citizenry, and they encouraged all manner of workers to participate in the distribution of this material. Shoeshine boys, shopkeepers, taxi drivers, and barbers passed out flyers to employees and clients. And when the government pressured all but the most radical television and radio stations to close, the anti-Reds formed their own "Network of Democracy," with over a hundred stations throughout the country. Partially bolstered by the Brazilian press, which supported their cause through editorials and regular columns, the anti-Red faction determinedly used the Communists' tactics against them.

The Church also took a public stand against Communist action. The archbishop of Rio de Janeiro, Cardinal de Barros Camara, launched a weekly radio address in which he encouraged the faithful to resist Communism by heeding the directives of Our Lady of Fatima. He exhorted people to pray the Rosary and do penance against the looming evil. The cardinal persisted even as President Goulart openly mocked him and insisted that only government control could spare the country from economic collapse. The more Goulart disparaged the Church and the Rosary, the more fervent the people became.

One night in mid-1962, a Brazilian woman named Doña Amelia Bastos was listening to her husband and other anti-Red leaders talk about the pressing Communist threat. Having heard enough, she made a bold move. "I suddenly decided that politics had become too important to be left entirely to the men," she would later say to Clarence Hall, senior editor for *Reader's Digest*.[29] The fifty-nine-year-old Bastos, whom Hall described as a "90-pound package of feminine energy," formed a group that came to be called the Campaign of Women for Democracy. The main requirement for membership was an agreement to pray the Rosary in large groups for the intention of blocking the planned Communist takeover.

The movement caught fire. At one of Bastos's rallies, in a town called Belo Horizonte, a group of twenty thousand women praying the Rosary managed to break up a pro-Communist rally. It was just the kind of victory the group needed to fan the flames of their faith and encourage them to continue the fight.

Like their male counterparts, the women used the Communists' tactics against them but added their feminine ingenuity to the mix. They met in parish halls with other women, whom they charged to form prayer cells in their homes with ten friends. These friends, in turn, would do the same. The cells served to inform, instruct, and inspire the women, as well as keep them alerted to upcoming events good and bad.

Additionally, the women used the phone to get hundreds of women to join them at public protest meetings. They put pressure on commercial firms to remove ads from the left-wing newspaper. They developed and disseminated their own literature filled with concerns specific to women. And they inspired the wives of union members to use their "feminine genius" to encourage their husbands to change sides. To fund their efforts, the women economized on their household budgets and asked well-heeled friends for donations.

§§ §§ §§

The audacious move of Amelia Bastos began to influence the public square. The women's efforts came to the attention of Cardinal Camara, who helped them recruit more than half a million women to march in Brazil's capital city of Sao Paulo while praying the Rosary for peace. They called their protest "March of the Family with God toward Freedom." Clutching their beads and raising anti-Communist banners, the women filled the streets of the city, praying the Rosary and imploring heaven: "Mother of God, preserve us from the fate and suffering of the martyred women of Cuba, Poland, Hungary, and other enslaved nations."[30]

During the march, a communist official tried to speak, and the women began rattling their Rosaries and praying so loudly that his voice was drowned out. He angrily stormed away.

In the days that followed, similar marches were held in major cities across the country. Regardless of the government's threats and the efforts of the Communist-controlled police, the women would not be cowed. They continued their solemn marches of prayer and petition. Heaven heard. The combination of growing sentiment against the Communists by the Brazilian military and the efforts of the Church forced Goulart to quit the country. On April 1, 1964, he fled to Uruguay, along with most of the officials he had appointed.

In large part, it was the women of Brazil who foiled the Communist takeover of their nation. "By the thousands, on a scale unmatched in Latin American history, housewives threw themselves into the struggle and more than any other force, they alerted the country."[31] Said one leader of the counter-revolution, "Without the women, we could never have halted Brazil's plunge toward communism."[32]

On April 2, the day after Goulart capitulated, the women planned yet another march, this one in thanksgiving to God. "This march will demonstrate to the world that this is a true People's Revolution, a marching plebiscite for real democracy," Doña Amelia Bastos said. And so they marched, more than a million strong, praying aloud as confetti rained down from the surrounding buildings. With the help of heaven, and relying upon the strong arm of the Blessed Virgin Mary, they had freed their nation without shedding a single drop of blood.[33]

WHAT ABOUT US?

In this our day and time, when "God is disappearing from the human horizon," when "humanity is losing its bearings, with increasingly evident destructive effects," and when "the faith is in danger of dying out like a flame which no longer has fuel,"[34] perhaps we would be well-advised to take a signal from those we have met in this chapter. Could the Holy Spirit be prompting us to pray the Rosary more consistently, with greater fervor, and with deeper intentionality? Might he even be asking us to begin a Rosary crusade in order to win back the culture for Jesus Christ? Upcoming chapters will give us insight on how we can increase our devotion to the Rosary, offer us ways to dig deeply into its mysteries to mine its treasures of grace, and help us to see why it is precisely the prayer we need at this moment in history.

Our next chapter starts us off on sure footing with the insight and wisdom of a hero of the Rosary from our own time, St. John Paul II.

A Rosary Story

At the close of each chapter, you will read the testimony of a person who has discovered the power and grace of the prayer of the Rosary. These men and women share their stories in order to encourage you to pray this prayer with greater dedication, confidence, and hope.

Why I Pray the Rosary: An Adoptive Mother's Story
HEIDI HESS SAXTON

When I became Catholic at the age of thirty, I did not immediately start praying the Rosary. I had always felt comfortable taking my prayers directly to God and didn't see the need to change that. It wasn't until I became a foster mother that I began to understand the benefits of cultivating a relationship with Jesus's mother and asking for her help when I needed it.

My husband and I adopted two of our foster children in 2005, when Chris was five and Sarah was three. The first three years were often chaotic and stressful, and I really struggled to keep my sense of humor and to treat the children with the kindness and gentleness they needed. Their fear and worry often made it difficult for all of us to sleep, and I spent hours rocking them in the dark or simply sitting nearby. The slow, meditative rhythm of the Rosary helped me stay calm and helped them drift into peaceful slumber on many nights.

I hadn't realized what an impression the prayers made on the children until many years later, when my eleven-year-old son had to be away from home for several months to get some special therapy. Whenever we came to visit Chris, he told us of how he would crawl under his bed at night with his Rosary beads and ask God to let him go home soon. While it was painful to be separated from him, I found it a great comfort to know that, when I could not be there to comfort him myself, he was experiencing the peace and comfort he needed in that moment, as he held those Rosary beads and talked to the Blessed Mother with the simple prayer of the heart.

Heidi Hess Saxton is the author of several books, including Lent with Saint Teresa of Calcutta: Daily Meditations *and* Raising Up Mommy: Virtues for Difficult Mothering Moments.

Why the Rosary? Why Now?

Today we have the greatest need of saints,
for whom we must assiduously implore God.[1]
—1985 Extraordinary Synod of Bishops

In 1976, Cardinal Karol Wojtyla, who two years later would become Pope John Paul II, visited the United States. While in this country, he made a stunning statement:

> We are now standing in the face of the greatest historical confrontation humanity has gone through. I do not think that wide circles of the American society, or wide circles of the Christian community, realize this fully. We are now facing the final confrontation between the Church and the anti-church, between the Gospel and the anti-gospel. This

confrontation lies within the plans of Divine Providence; it is a trial which the whole Church must take up.[2]

This statement was prophetic in both senses of the word. Pope John Paul II had the wisdom to see the temporal moment from the eternal perspective and the supernatural gaze to see its future implications.

In 1976, Western civilization was rapidly losing its Judeo-Christian heritage. Secular humanism was becoming the religion of the masses. Moral relativism was silencing consciences and forming hearts. The Church herself was in a state of confusion due to the misapplication of the teachings of the Second Vatican Council. Long-held principles and institutions that had shaped our collective moral compass were in the crosshairs.

In a particular way, family life was under severe attack in the United States, Canada, and Western Europe. An atmosphere of permissiveness and sexual license had taken hold of the post–World War II generation. Contraception was in general use by women, including Catholics. Abortion had been legalized, as had no-fault divorce. The Gay Pride Movement and the removal of homosexuality from the American Psychiatric Association's list of mental disorders indicated a pressured push toward codification of the homosexual lifestyle. And as the moral fabric of Western civilization began to unravel, the media, which championed all of these social ills, reached their influential zenith.

The history is clear. In 1976, things were bleak, and the horizon looked bleaker for those values that have always been at the heart of Holy Mother Church and Western civilization in general. Indeed, as Cardinal Karol Wojtyla gave his chilling prediction of a coming confrontation between the Gospel and the anti-gospel, the Church and the anti-church, he was reading the signs of the times. He was a keen observer of contemporary events and a man whose own life experience prepared him to see more deeply than most.

Karol Wojtyla lived through the Nazi occupation of his beloved Poland, and he knew well the face of evil and the trial and tribulation of war. He was an educated man, a priest of the Church who studied under Father Reginald Garrigou-Lagrange, the great Dominican theologian of the twentieth century. Wojtyla graduated from the Angelicum with a doctorate in sacred theology.

But Cardinal Wojtyla was far more than a wise scholar. He was a man of piety and devotion, a contemplative of heart and soul. He had a great devotion to the Blessed Mother and was consecrated to Jesus through her according to the spiritual path advanced by St. Louis de Montfort. His innate gifts—brilliance, congeniality, a charismatic personality, wit, an undeniable love for others—found fulfillment in his life of prayer. They were shot through with the grace of God. Add to all of this the prophetic gift of the Holy Spirit, and you have the prophet who was Karol Wojtyla.

His message during the bicentennial year of the United States not only assessed the contemporary culture from an eternal perspective but also predicted events to come. He indicated there would be an unprecedented showdown—a final confrontation of epic proportions—between the Church and the anti-church, the Gospel and the anti-gospel. This confrontation, he indicated, would lead to a great trial.

One iteration of his now famous quote includes these words:

> We must be prepared to undergo great trials in the not-too-distant future; trials that will require us to be ready to give up even our lives, and a total gift of self to Christ and for Christ. Through your prayers and mine, it is possible to alleviate this tribulation, but it is no longer possible to avert it.... How many times has the renewal of the Church been brought about in blood! It will not be different this time.[3]

Strong words, to be sure, but not words without hope. This trial, the future pope said, "lies within the plans of Divine Providence," and it can be alleviated through prayer.

A REMEDY FOR SOCIETY

Two years after this visit to America, Cardinal Wojtyla was elected to the Chair of Peter, and he selected the name John Paul II. In his addresses and official writings, shades of his 1976 statement in America recur and often seem corrective for the moral ills that plague contemporary culture.

Take, for example, his Wednesday papal audiences. Beginning in September of 1979 and continuing until November of 1984, Pope John Paul II delivered 129 teachings on what has come to be known as the Theology of the Body. These addresses were a response to the distorted attitudes and notions about human sexuality spawned by the sexual revolution, which saw the body simply as an object for pleasure and gratification. The Holy Father sought to replace this cultural perspective with the rich understanding of the body's intrinsic meaning, value, and personal dimension. He covered a wide range of topics, emphasizing the beauty of sexual differentiation, the complementarity between man and woman, and love as the gift of self. These watershed teachings reflect his intellect and largesse as a philosopher and theologian but also his shepherd's heart.

In his 1988 Apostolic Exhortation on the Vocation and Mission of the Lay Faithful in the Church and in the World, Pope John Paul II speaks with particular urgency about the need to repair the society of man. He reminds the faithful of their duty, sacred trust, and fundamental call to holiness. He tells us that because "a new state of affairs" exists within the Church as well as within "social, economic, political, and cultural life," the action of the lay faithful is absolutely urgent. Lack of commitment is unacceptable, he tells us: *"It is not permissible for anyone to remain idle"* (*Christifidelis Laici*, 3).

The pope encourages us to "accept the gospel in faith and to proclaim it in word and deed," to let its "newness and power...shine out" in our families as well as our social life. In the midst of the difficulties, trials, and contradictions of the present day, he exhorts the faithful to patiently and courageously express their "hope of future glory even 'through the framework of their secular life.'"[4]

The Holy Father reminded the faithful of the urgency expressed by the 1985 Extraordinary Synod:

Men and women saints have always been the source and origin of renewal in the most difficult circumstances in the Church's history. Today we have the greatest need of saints whom we must assiduously beg God to raise up. (*CL*, 16)

The pope made clear, in a 1985 address to the European bishops, the qualities these saints must possess. "We need heralds of the Gospel today who are experts in humanity," he proclaimed, "who know the depths of the heart of man today, who share in his hopes and joys, his worries and his sadness, and at the same time are contemplatives, in love with God."

"For this," he says, "new saints are needed. The great evangelizers…have been saints. We must implore God to increase the spirit of holiness in the Church and to send us new saints to evangelize today's world."[5]

Pope John Paul II was unrelenting in his quest to preach the truth to a world increasingly hardened against it, and time and again he called the people of the Church to do the same—even if it meant persecution or death. He spoke about the new types of religious persecution that had developed in the twentieth century and the courage necessary to stand firm in the faith. He encouraged the people of God to pray for all of those who face injustice and the suppression of human rights and freedoms and to work on their behalf. He reminded the faithful that "the supreme trial of martyrdom has often been demanded of Christians,"[6] and he held aloft for them as icons the martyrs of antiquity.[7] He exhorted the faithful to follow the saints' examples of holiness of life and their witness to the faith, informing them *"the Church has become once again a Church of martyrs."*[8]

CALL TO HOLINESS

Perhaps one of the pope's most arresting exhortations to embrace holiness of life, persecution, and the great witness of martyrdom (should it be necessary) is in his Papal Bull of Indiction of the Jubilee Year 2000, *Incarnationis Mysterium*, promulgated on November 29, 1998. In it, the prophetic voice rings clear. Pope John Paul II once again recalls the great witness of the martyrs and then states,

> The believer who has seriously pondered his Christian vocation, including what Revelation has to say about the possibility of martyrdom, cannot exclude it from his own life's horizon....
>
> Martyrdom is the most eloquent proof of the truth of the faith, for faith can give a human face even to the most violent of deaths and show its beauty even in the midst of the most atrocious persecutions.
>
> ...In the hearts of the faithful, may admiration for their martyrdom be matched by the desire to follow their example, with God's grace, should circumstances require it.[9]

As the Church entered the third millennium, evangelization imbued with holiness of life, along with the exhortation to martyrdom in all its forms, continued to be a key aspect of John Paul II's teaching for the lay faithful. Take, for example, his address at the Prayer Vigil for World Youth Day 2000 in Rome, Italy. After providing the young people with an exegesis on Matthew 16:15 (Jesus's question to His apostles,

"But who do you say I am?"), he talked with them about the questioning of faith that is often part of the maturation process both chronologically and spiritually. Then he spoke with them about the need to be a witness to Jesus Christ and the "new martyrdom" to which it could lead.

He reminded the young people that today they must "go against the tide in order to follow the divine Master." While they may not be called to shed their blood, he told them, they "will certainly be asked to be faithful to Christ!" This, the pope said, is a "faithfulness to be lived in the circumstances of everyday life."[10]

At the closing Mass for the Seventeenth World Youth Day in 2002, in Toronto, Canada, the Holy Father again exhorted young people to be the *salt* in the world of man, to stand firm, and to not lose hope. Though he was aged and frail, his words were strong. He sought to instill in the hearts and minds of the young a vision of who they can be in Christ Jesus:

> The "spirit of the world" offers many false illusions and parodies of happiness. There is perhaps no darkness deeper than the darkness that enters young people's souls when false prophets extinguish in them the light of faith and hope and love. The greatest deception, and the deepest source of unhappiness, is the illusion of finding life by excluding God, of finding freedom by excluding moral truths and personal responsibility....
>
> The world you are inheriting is a world which needs to be touched and healed by the beauty and richness of God's love. It needs witnesses to that love. The world needs salt.

It needs you—to be the salt of the earth and the light of the world....

Do not let that hope die! Stake your lives on it! We are not the sum of our weaknesses and failures; we are the sum of the Father's love for us and our real capacity to become the image of his Son.[11]

THE SAINT MAKER

This call to commitment and action coupled with holiness of life persists through the corpus of St. John Paul II's teaching. His apostolic letters, encyclicals, exhortations, and addresses encourage the lay faithful to engage the culture with faith-filled perseverance and hope. And he continued not only to reference the saints of the past but to give the Church new ones as well.

"The Saint Maker," as Pope John Paul II was fondly called, canonized a record number of 482 saints and beatified another 1,327 men and women. Nearly 280 of the saints were laity.

Of the beatified, at least 920 were martyrs.[12] These men and women from a variety of walks of life evidenced the virtues the Holy Father hoped to inspire in others. He elevated these men and women to the altar as champions for our day and time.

But perhaps what spoke most deeply to the hearts of the multitudes was Pope John Paul II's own life witness. From the vitality of his early years to the disabilities of his later, he embraced each turn with holy zeal, love of Christ, dedication to the Church, love for God's people, and union with Christ's cross.

This witness was magnificently evident when Mehmet Ali Agca's bullet threatened the pope's life on the Feast of Our Lady of Fatima in 1981. Upon his recovery, the Holy Father stunned the world through a profound act of mercy. He visited Agca in prison and offered him forgiveness. This action, so reminiscent of Jesus's loving action from the cross—"Father, forgive them; for they know not what they do"—was a sign and witness for all. United to Christ, the pope embraced the cross and its suffering. This witness defined the type of martyrdom he invited his flock to desire.

Though Pope John Paul II could have experienced the red rose of martyrdom through the assassination attempt of Mehmet Ali Agca, this was not God's plan for him. The plan was to offer him the rose of white martyrdom—the type of self-sacrifice that comes through a loving response to the trials of daily life, suffered in union with the Passion of Christ. In this regard, the entirety of John Paul II's life might be a prophetic word—one that articulates both the certain challenge of the modern Christian experience as well as the antidote to it: redemptive suffering.[13]

Cardinal Stanislaw Dziwisz, Pope John Paul II's close personal friend and collaborator, gives witness to the word of the Holy Father's life. He remarked, "the Pope's blood was shed…and the Pope came close to martyrdom by blood," and afterward, "his pontificate was marked by another kind of martyrdom: hard work, sacrifice being consumed by Christ and his cause, for which the Savior of man came to earth."[14] The cardinal recalled:

I stayed with him until the end, until his last breath.... The death and funeral of John Paul II in themselves became an emotional catechesis for the entire world.

...The holiness of the Pope is the synthesis of what he was, what he was able to achieve.[15]

Pope St. John Paul II's words were the echo of his life, and his life was a portrait of his soul. In his early years, he possessed the dynamism of a man coming to full stature in Christ Jesus. In his later years, he was that man of full stature conformed to the image of Jesus Christ crucified. From whence had such grace come?

SON OF MARY

To be sure, Karol Jozef Wojtyla was entrusted to good and holy parents who raised him in the faith and taught him how to live a life of faith. Both had a profound effect on him, though he lost his mother at the age of eight. His father, Karol Senior, was known in their town of Wadowice as a "just man," and he believed it was his duty to raise his sons likewise. John Paul II would later recount that his father was a man of "constant prayer" and that his example was "in a way my first seminary, a kind of domestic seminary."[16] The two would read the Bible together and pray the Rosary regularly.

These two devotions helped to hold the young Karol firm as the realities of his day and time pressed upon him. He was nineteen years old and serving Mass in the Krakow cathedral when the first bombs fell on his native country, September 1, 1939. A university student at the time, Karol and his father were among the refugees who fled the invading army, returning some weeks later to a land that had been transformed. Swastikas flew from flagpoles, and all of the best shops in town boasted signs that warned, "For Germans only." The university had been looted, its libraries wrecked, its laboratories destroyed, and its faculty members arrested. History reports that 18 percent of Poland's thirty-five million people would die in World War II.

The Third Reich did not prize education, at least for its occupied countries. The Germans mandated that every male between the ages of fourteen and sixty have a job. And so it was that the pope-in-the-making worked as a messenger in a restaurant and then shoveled limestone in frigid temperatures at a chemical company, all the while giving testimony to his life of faith. George Weigel, the Holy Father's biographer, writes that fellow workers "remember Karol Wojtyla praying on his knees at the Borek Fałecki plant, unafraid of ridicule and seemingly able to tune out the racket around him to concentrate on his conversation with God."[17] In the midst of suffering and strife, God was about a great work.

Karol began to study the works of the great Saint Louis Marie Grignion de Montfort. He was captivated. In an address to the Eighth International Mariological Colloquium in Rome in 2000, Pope John Paul II noted that he had read the saint's treatise on *True Devotion to Mary* a number of times.

I then realized that I could not exclude the Mother of the Lord from my life without neglecting the will of

God-the-Trinity, who wanted to "begin and complete" the great mysteries of salvation history with the responsible and faithful collaboration of the humble Handmaid of Nazareth.[18]

The effect of this work and its spirituality had a profound influence on his priesthood.

My life reached a decisive turning point when I read this book. I say "turning point," although in fact it was part of an interior journey that coincided with my secret preparation for the priesthood. It was then that this singular book fell into my hands, one of those books of which one can say that simply "having read" it is not enough. I remember carrying it with me for a long time, even to the soda works, to the point that there were lime stains all over its beautiful cover. I realized right away that there was something fundamental contained within that baroque style. From that point on, the devotion of my childhood and even of my adolescence to the Mother of God gave way to a new attitude, a devotion rising from the depths of my faith, as if from the very heart of the trinitarian and Christological reality.[19]

And so it was that in 1978, when he was elected pope, John Paul II consecrated his pontificate to Mary, the Mother of God. In a letter he wrote to the Montfort religious family on the occasion of the 160th anniversary of the publication of St. Louis de Montfort's treatise on *True Devotion* to the Blessed Virgin, he talked about his motto, *Totus Tuus.* He stated that his episcopal coat of arms symbolically illustrates

John 19:25–27, in which Jesus from the cross entrusts His mother to the beloved disciple, John.

As Holy Mother Church teaches, St. John represents all of the brethren of Christ who come to him via baptism. Therefore, when Jesus bequeaths the Blessed Mother to St. John, he is bequeathing her to all the baptized as well. She becomes our mother, too.

St. John Paul II also stated that the motto *Totus Tuus* was inspired by the teaching of St. Louis de Montfort and expressed his "belonging" to Jesus through Mary. The Pope wrote, "These two words express total belonging to Jesus through Mary... 'I am all Yours, and all that I have is Yours, O most loving Jesus, through Mary, your most holy Mother.'"[20]

EVANGELIZER OF THE ROSARY

For John Paul II, the Montfort prayer of consecration was not one prayer among many; it was a way of life, a spirituality that imbued the way he saw the world and the way he lived in the world. And so it is no surprise that the Rosary held pride of place in his spiritual life. St. Louis de Montfort was a major proponent of the Rosary, encouraging all of his spiritual sons and daughters in its recitation. For the Holy Father, this was but a continuation of the long-held devotional practice he began as a child. In his apostolic letter *Rosarium Virginis Mariae*, he tells the lay faithful that the Rosary accompanied him "in moments of joy and in moments of difficulty." To it he "entrusted any number of concerns," and he "always found comfort" in it (*RVM*, 2).

In this same letter, he reminds the faithful that scarcely two weeks after his election to the See of Peter, he stated that the Rosary was his "favorite prayer" and a "marvelous prayer." In fact, he tells us, so important was this prayer to him that he set the first year of his pontificate "within the daily rhythm of the Rosary," and he wished to do the same with the twenty-fifth year of his service as the Successor of Peter (*RVM*, 2).

Pope John Paul II knew the power of the Rosary through his own life of prayer, his personal experience of its efficacy, its history in the life of the Church, and the witness of holy men and women throughout time. He saw it, at the dawn of the third millennium, as "a prayer of great significance, destined to bring forth a harvest of holiness" (*RVM*, 1). He also saw it as a means to peace in the wake of the terrorist attacks of September 11, 2001, and as a way to quell the menacing "forces of disintegration on both the ideological and practical planes" that threaten the institution of the family (*RVM*, 6). He saw it as a way to make progress in the new evangelization and to foster "the *art of prayer*," which leads to authentic Christian witness (*RVM*, 5).

The Holy Father ends his letter with a heart-wrenching appeal shot through with urgency. Perhaps in 2002 he was seeing the actualization of the prophetic word he had given some twenty-six years earlier while visiting the United States. Perhaps he realized that the great historical confrontation that humanity was facing then was now engaged. Perhaps he saw the demons of "anti-church" and "anti-gospel" dressed in battle gear and waging war. Perhaps he knew that the primordial battle was being fought by the powers of darkness with particular efficacy in the contemporary moment. And perhaps he knew that the only weapon to save the day is the one that saved so many in days past—the Rosary.

And so the pope beseeches the Church: "*Confidently take up the Rosary once again.* Rediscover the Rosary in the light of Scripture, in harmony with the Liturgy, and in the context of your daily lives.... May this appeal of mine not go unheard!" (*RVM*, 43)

The pope leads the charge in dedication to the Rosary. He ends his letter with a quote from Blessed Bartolo Longo, a nineteenth-century Satanist priest who converted to Catholicism, became a third order Dominican, and spearheaded construction of the Basilica to Our Lady of the Most Holy Rosary in Pompeii. There a painting featuring Our Lady, St. Dominic, and St. Catherine of Siena has been credited with many miracles.

> At the start of the twenty-fifth year of my Pontificate, I entrust this Apostolic Letter to the loving hands of the Virgin Mary, *prostrating myself in spirit before her image in the splendid Shrine built for her by Blessed Bartolo Longo,* the apostle of the Rosary. I willingly make my own the touching words with which he concluded his well-known *Supplication to the Queen of the Holy Rosary:* "O Blessed Rosary of Mary, sweet chain which unites us to God, bond of love which unites us to the angels, tower of salvation against the assaults of Hell, safe port in our universal shipwreck, we will never abandon you. You will

be our comfort in the hour of death: yours our final kiss as life ebbs away. And the last word from our lips will be your sweet name, O Queen of the Rosary of Pompeii, O dearest Mother, O Refuge of Sinners, O Sovereign Consoler of the Afflicted. May you be everywhere blessed, today and always, on earth and in heaven." (*RVM*, 43)

Indeed, we are in a battle. But where did this battle originate? What is the history of these demons of treachery, and why is Mary so effective against them? That's what we'll consider in the upcoming chapters.

A Rosary Story
A Priest's Spiritual Weapon
FR. DONALD CALLOWAY, MIC

One of the first things I did after converting to Catholicism was learn how to pray the Rosary. I also read *The Secret of the Rosary* by St. Louis de Montfort. I'm convinced that praying a daily Rosary helped me discern a vocation to the priesthood. This practice also inspired me to write two of my own books on the Rosary: *Rosary Gems: Daily Wisdom on the Holy Rosary* and *Champions of the Rosary: The History and Heroes of a Spiritual Weapon*.

For me, one of the most fascinating aspects of the Rosary is that Our Lady entrusted it to a priest, St. Dominic, the founder of the Dominicans. When Mary gave him the Rosary, she told him that it was to be a spiritual weapon against theological error, sin, and the devil.

The century of St. Dominic—the thirteenth century—was a time of chivalry, knights, and swords. The Mercedarians, another religious order founded during that time, even wore a sword on the left side of their habit. When Mary entrusted the Rosary to her chosen priest, St. Dominic may have done something similar. He eventually required his band of preachers to wear the spiritual sword of the Rosary on the left side of their habit.

Though the Rosary is for everyone, the greatest champions of the Rosary throughout history have been priests—including founders of religious orders, bishops, and popes. In fact, one of the main reasons St. Louis de Montfort wrote *The Secret of the Rosary* was to encourage his brother priests in this devotion.

Every priest is ordained to proclaim the sacred mysteries of Christ. A priest without a Rosary is like a knight without a sword. With this heavenly weapon, a priest can defeat falsehood, conquer evil, and win innumerable souls for Jesus Christ!

Fr. Donald Calloway, a member of the Congregation of Marian Fathers of the Immaculate Conception of the Most Blessed Virgin Mary, is a popular speaker, a pilgrimage leader, and the author of several books on Mary and Divine Mercy.

Chapter Three

Before Time Began

THE PRIMORDIAL BATTLE

And a great portent appeared in heaven, a woman
clothed with the sun, with the moon under her feet,
and on her head a crown of twelve stars; she was
with child and she cried out in her pangs of birth,
in anguish for delivery.

—REVELATION 12:1–2

When all signs indicate a naval warship is in peril, an
announcement is made and a signal given that everyone
aboard the ship is to move to his or her assigned station
without delay. Within a matter of seconds, every station is
fully manned, ammunition is ready for loading, and guns and
guided missile launchers are set to go. "General quarters,"
as this announcement is known, is not to be ignored. The
Department of Defense Dictionary of Military and Associated

Terms defines it as "a condition of readiness when naval action is imminent."[1]

There is no drill or condition of readiness more important than general quarters. This call to battle stations affects every single person on board. Everyone down to the last person has a vital duty and a life-or-death role to play. Adrenaline rushes, the heartbeat accelerates, and the fruit of training kicks into gear. Survival of life and mission are at stake.

The same is true in the Christian life. Recognize it or not, our life on earth is a warfare (see *CCC*, 409), and every day and age from the beginning of time tells the story of dour combat with diabolic forces, a war between good and evil. This battle originated in the heavens before the dawn of humanity but was not confined there. It spilled onto the earth, placing all generations of humanity in a perpetual state of general quarters.

Recall that St. Peter tells us, "Be sober, be watchful. Your adversary the devil prowls around like a roaring lion, seeking some one to devour" (1 Peter 5:8). St. Paul writes: "For we are not contending against flesh and blood, but against the principalities, against the powers, against the world rulers of this present darkness, against the spiritual hosts of wickedness in the heavenly places" (Ephesians 6:12).

Today, as St. John Paul II said, we are engaged in a confrontation of epic proportion. And as soldiers of Christ, it is our job to respond. God has chosen us for this time to be the men and women who preserve and protect that which is God-honoring and who reclaim that which has been lost.

Our mission, as the Council Fathers told us, requires "the penetrating and perfecting of the temporal order through the spirit of the Gospel."[2] Like the response of our military counterparts to general quarters, we must man the battle stations, make ready the high-powered artillery, and use our weapon— the Holy Rosary of the Blessed Virgin Mary. Consider the words of Pope Pius XI, who like his predecessor, Pope Leo XIII, saw the darkness making its advance:

> The Rosary is a powerful weapon to put the demons to flight and to keep oneself from sin... If you desire peace in your hearts, in your homes, and in your country, assemble each evening to recite the Rosary. Let not even one day pass without saying it, no matter how burdened you may be with many cares and labors.[3]

But there is one more thing: If we hope to be victorious in the battle against the world, the flesh, and the devil, we need to know ourselves as well as the enemy and his tactics and strategies. As the ancient Chinese philosopher and military general, Sun Tzu said in his classic work *The Art of War*, anyone who does not know himself nor his enemy, will succumb in every battle.[4] Therefore, let's return to the beginnings of the struggle. There we will discover our nemesis, his wiles and ways, his cohorts and minions, and why we are in his crosshairs. Then we will be able to confidently give the rallying cry of the soldier moving into battle as he responds to the orders of his commander: "HUA!," heard, understood, acknowledged.

INFINITE LOVE

St. John begins his Gospel with the words, "In the beginning was the Word, and the Word was with God, and the Word was God. He was in the beginning with God; all things were made through him, and without him was not anything made that was made" (John 1:1–3).

Ponder these words for just a moment. Who is this God, and what defines Him? What was made "through him," and what does His creation have to do with the enemy, the battle, and you and me?

First, this God is a Trinity of Persons—God the Father, God the Son, and God the Holy Spirit—and although each Person is separate and distinct, the Divine Persons are "one in being." The defining reality of this divine communion of Persons is love. St. John sums it up simply when he states, "God is love" (1 John 4:16).

Theologians tell us that so great is the mutuality of the love of God the Father and God the Son that from it "proceeds" or "spirates" the Third Person of the Blessed Trinity, the Holy Spirit. Love, then, is a life-giving dynamic that replicates itself through self-donative action.

Love, true love, gives completely and totally without reservation, generously and willingly without condition. Love desires to go out of itself for another, who in turn will love in a corresponding act of selfless giving. Love cannot be coerced. It cannot be forced. It cannot be mandated. Its essence is mutual surrender, gift, offering. It is, as St. John Paul II states, an act of total self-donation.[5]

Now, the first few verses of St. John's Gospel tell us that in the beginning, everything came into being through the Word of God, who was God. Everything came into being through the life-giving dynamic of the one who is Love. God is never-ending and unchanging. As it was then, it is now.

This Trinity of Persons, the infinitude of love, seeks to share the life-giving dynamic of Their loving union with others—to "go outward" to others who will love back in the same self-donative way. This is gratuitous action on God's part. Being the infinitude of love, the Divine Persons have no need of more love, but They seek to share with others Their divine pleasure. And so God created the heavens and the earth and beings with whom He might share His very life.

The Angelic Hosts

The beings God created first in order to share His love were spiritual beings, persons, whom we call angels. All of the angels who would ever exist were created in this one manifestation of God's loving action. St. Thomas Aquinas tells us, in his *Summa Theologiae*, that no two angels are alike, and each one is its own species.[6]

The angels vary in distinctive ways. Monsignor Paul Glenn, in *A Tour of the Summa*, explains St. Thomas's teaching that the angels possess immense power and intelligence; however, no two angels have the same amount of power and knowledge. The power and knowledge given to an angel correlate to the service it renders to God.[7] The categorization of angels in terms of knowledge and power is called the nine choirs of angels.

St. Thomas Aquinas divided the nine choirs of angels into three hierarchies, each of which contains three orders, which are also hierarchical in structure. The proximity of these angels to God is what serves as the basis of this division. God placed seraphim, cherubim, and thrones in the first hierarchy; in the second hierarchy, He placed dominations, virtues, and powers; in the third, God placed principalities, archangels, and angels. Each hierarchy and each order has its own designated mission, and each angel within that hierarchy or order is endowed with the power and intelligence necessary to complete its mission.[8]

In addition to power and intelligence, God bestowed upon the angels yet another gift. As has been noted, His purpose for creation is to share the divine pleasure of the Trinitarian Love with others. But love cannot be coerced, forced, or mandated. God does not want a robotic relationship with His creatures. Rather, He wants them to love Him in the same self-donative way as He loves—freely. He desired the angels to have the freedom to choose to love, to trust, and to follow His divine plan. And so, to the angels' power and intelligence, God added free will.

But would the angels choose the way of God, or would they refuse to obey? Their love and loyalty would need to be proven. There would be a test of fidelity by which each would decide conclusively for or against God. The decision would be irreversible, with no second chance.

While at first thought this may seem harsh, remember that the angels were created with the full knowledge they needed for their hierarchy and order. This means that the angelic decision to choose for or against God was made without ignorance and with full culpability. Each angel knew precisely what he was choosing, and he chose freely, without compromise.

The Test

While the exact nature of the angelic test remains a mystery, many saints and theologians have offered cogent and reasoned speculations.

The writings of St. Maximilian Kolbe indicate that at the heart of the rebellion of the angels is the mystery of the Incarnation. "The Word became flesh," entering His own creation in the fullness of time, by means of a woman whom God selected. St. Maximilian tells us that this woman would be known as the Mother of God and heralded as Queen of Heaven and Earth. She would be endowed "with perfect form, immaculate, with no slightest taint of sin, a creature who would reflect his own divine qualities in the most perfect degree possible for a created nature."[9]

It suited God to reveal His desire and His vision about this creature with the angelic hosts, the saint says, so they might rejoice with Him and share in His divine pleasure. So too, He sought the proof of their love, loyalty, and obedience to Him in this regard and all others.

While St. John the Evangelist was exiled on the island of Patmos, God granted him an amazing vision. Could it be that John saw the angelic test? Here is what Scripture records:

> And a great portent appeared in heaven, a woman clothed
> with the sun, with the moon under her feet, and on her
> head a crown of twelve stars; she was with child and she
> cried out in her pangs of birth, in anguish for delivery.
> (Revelation 12:1)

The angels knew that this woman was to be their queen, and
she would bring forth a son who would be their King. St.
Maximilian tells us that though many of the angels hailed
their future Sovereign with joy and acclaim and paid homage
to their future queen, some of them, led by Lucifer, refused
to submit. Their pride was too great.

The saint writes, "To pay homage to a woman seemed to
them a derogation to their dignity; they fell into pride and
refused to go along with God's will." He comments, "Their
crime had all the characteristics of a mortal sin, since they fully
consented to what they did." And for this, "from being angels
they became demons forever."[10]

In his book *The Angels in Catholic Teaching and Tradition*,
Fr. Pascale Parente writes about this moment:

> Pride is a false estimation of oneself; it is a lie, just as
> humility is truth. Pride is the root of disobedience, the
> instigator of sedition and rebellions. In that period of
> probation one of the supreme Angels recognized his
> exceeding power, beauty and knowledge but failed to give
> thanks and glory to God. He became envious and intol-
> erant of God's supreme dominion, and thereby he consti-
> tuted himself as the adversary of God: he became *Satan*.
> Like a sinister flash of lightning, his evil mind was made
> manifest in the spirit world. Because of his exalted position

many Angels followed him in his mad campaign of hate and rebellion. It was then that a cry and a challenge was heard in the heavens, and a leader was seen to rise from the lowest Hierarchy, from the Choir of the Archangels. His battle cry: "*Who is like God?*" was his mighty weapon and it became, later, his own name: *Michael*.[11]

THE WAR

The supreme angel who led the rebellion was the seraphim Lucifer, whose name means "Light Bringer." This indicates that he may well have been the highest ranking of all the seraphim, the choir of angels closest to God. Beautiful, strong, and intelligent, he reflected the majesty of God himself. But the moment pride and rebellion entered his mind, a stunning transformation befell him. He became, according to St. John the Evangelist, a terrifying dragon.

> And another portent appeared in heaven; behold, a great red dragon, with seven heads and ten horns, and seven diadems upon his heads. His tail swept down a third of the stars of heaven, and cast them to the earth. And the dragon stood before the woman who was about to bear a child, that he might devour her child when she brought it forth; she brought forth a male child, one who is to rule all the nations with a rod of iron, but her child was caught up to God and to his throne, and the woman fled into the wilderness, where she has a place prepared by God, in which to be nourished for one thousand two hundred and sixty days. (Revelation 12:3–6)

St. John tells us what happened next:

> Now war arose in heaven, Michael and his angels fighting
> against the dragon; and the dragon and his angels fought,
> but they were defeated and there was no longer any place
> for them in heaven. And the great dragon was thrown
> down, that ancient serpent, who is called the Devil and
> Satan, the deceiver of the whole world—he was thrown
> down to the earth, and his angels were thrown down with
> him. (Revelation 12:7–9)

Thus, we see the test of and the subsequent fall of the angels.
However, the battle was not over. The vitriol and malevolence
of Satan and his minions did not end once they were hurled
down to earth. They persisted in their diabolic plan.

St. Maximilian tells us that the demons have never forgotten
the vision of the Immaculata. Nor have they forgotten that
she was their stumbling block. He writes, "Because of this
the demons' anger flared up against her, an infernal hatred
just like that which they entertain toward God himself, whose
faithful image she is."[12]

Revelation tells us that this *infernal hatred* extends to the
woman's *offspring*: "Then the dragon was angry with the
woman, and went off to make war on the rest of her offspring,
on those who keep the commandments of God and bear testimony to Jesus" (Revelation 12:17). Here we discover what
the primordial battle has to do with you and me. An event in
the heavenlies, before the dawn of civilization, is not bound
to that moment; rather, it entered into the life of man and

persists through the ages, with deleterious effect on all the *offspring* of the woman.

As baptized Christians, you and I are the offspring of the woman, the brethren of her Son, Jesus Christ. Therefore, in this moment of man's history, the battle is ours. Do we battle alone? What provision has God made for us? To answer this question, we must look to the beginning of humanity, which we will do in the next chapter.

A Rosary Story
The Rosary and the Vocation to Love
Fr. Wade Menezes, CPM

In his landmark apostolic exhortation *Familiaris Consortio* (The Role of the Christian Family in the Modern World), Pope St. John Paul II states, "Love is…the fundamental and innate vocation of every human being" (11). Simply put, because "God is love" (1 John 4:16) and because the human person is made in God's image and likeness (Genesis 1:26–27), the human person is indeed called to love.

The Rosary is a prayer that bolsters this important truth. It is a prayer of love precisely because it teaches us how to love in the circumstances of everyday human life. Its four sets of mysteries together represent a complete rhythm of human life and a blueprint by which to live that life well, in love toward both God and neighbor.

The Joyful Mysteries help us acquire and live well the virtues needed for family life. The Luminous Mysteries, as they focus specifically on Our Lord's three years of public life, help us see how we must carry out our Christian vocation and mission in the modern world. The Sorrowful Mysteries teach us how to faithfully cope with any sufferings and tribulations that might enter our lives. And the Glorious Mysteries help us focus on the goal for which God has created us—namely, eternal salvation, eternal beatitude, the beatific vision, life with God forever in heaven.

As a Father of Mercy priest, my primary apostolate is to serve as an itinerant missionary who preaches the truth as it is revealed to us through Sacred Scripture, Tradition, and the Magisterium and upheld by the Sacred Deposit of Faith. Preaching the truth *with love* is a sacred duty I don't take lightly. The Rosary assists me greatly in this regard.

Since my early years, the Rosary has been a driving force behind all that I hold dear: my love for the Blessed Trinity, my love for our Blessed Mother, my love for the saints and angels, my love for family, my love for neighbor, and my love for my vocation as a priest. With its twenty mysteries geared toward the economy of salvation, the Rosary keeps me on track and focused, with the desire to demonstrate love in all the circumstances that life presents, including unexpected twists and turns and, yes, even sufferings.

My prayer is that the Rosary will likewise become a driving force for you and for all who come into contact with it. May we pray it faithfully and lovingly, regardless of vocation or state in life. This is crucial in a day and age in which we pray that a culture of life may overcome a culture of death. With the Rosary in our hands, its prayers on our lips, and its meditations on our minds, may we courageously echo to the world the solemn truth that Pope St. John Paul II taught so well: Indeed, *love is...the fundamental and innate vocation of every human being.*

Fr. Wade Menezes, CPM, is the assistant general of the Fathers of Mercy, a missionary preaching congregation based in Auburn, Kentucky. He has hosted several series on EWTN (Eternal Word Television Network).

Chapter Four

In the Beginning

THE GARDEN, MAN, AND WOMAN

Bring my sons from afar
and my daughters from the end of the earth,
every one who is called by my name,
whom I created for my glory,
whom I formed and made.

—ISAIAH 43:6–7

No doubt you are familiar with the account of the earth's creation (see Genesis 1—2). It speaks to the orderly and intentional way in which God created the world, as well as to the splendor with which He created the two creatures who would manifest his divine life.

In these first two chapters of Genesis, we discover that God's creative plan moved from the inanimate to the animate, from smaller life forms to larger. He began by separating the earth from the heavens, placing light in the sky, and gathering the waters into one place to reveal dry land. Then He created vegetation—plant life and trees that bear fruit. He populated the waters with sea creatures, the sky with birds, and the dry land with legged creatures. Everything about the creation of the world indicated that God was preparing a place for a creature who would be his masterpiece and take dominion over the world He had created.

And so it was. Out of the dust of the earth, God formed man in His image, after His likeness (Genesis 1:26). He breathed life into the man's nostrils, and the man became a living being (Genesis 2:7). The man was called Adam. And just as God had a plan and a mission for the angels, so too did God have a plan and a mission for the man.

God would entrust to man the whole of His creation. Man was to care for it and cultivate it, to protect it and preserve it. He would be the steward of it, responsible to God for it. And through this work, the man would grow in his masculinity, imaging God as protector, provider, and leader.

And just as God tested the angels, so too would He test the man's love and fidelity.

We can picture Adam as he beholds the plentitude and diversity of the creation God is entrusting to him. His eyes reflect wonder and amazement as he drinks in the marvels of the world God has created. Gratitude fills his heart. Perhaps a passion to explore this land excites him, and the desire to discover the "more" of it propels him to take his first steps into its expanse. Maybe he experiences a growing certainty of God's provision for him as one foot follows the other.

Adam sees all kinds of creatures on the earth and in the sky: crawling things, things that stride upon the land, flying things. Other creatures jump from the rivers and streams, arc in the sky, and drop back down to silvery depths. All of these creatures are unlike him, and their differences fascinate and inspire him.

Curiosity wells up in Adam. What are these creatures? What do they do? Why do they exist? All that he beholds captivates and thrills him. Soon God will invite Adam to participate in His divine leadership by giving names to these creatures He has made.

Perhaps God pointed out some of the geographic characteristics of the garden to Adam as they walked along in the breezy time of the day.[1] Perhaps He indicated a certain type of vegetation and told the man about it. Perhaps He called his attention to this plant, that vine, a fruit-bearing tree, a berry-producing shrub. Perhaps God invited Adam to sample some of creation's delicacies. He may have told Adam that all of these were for his consumption and sustenance and benefit.

Maybe God, in His fatherly wisdom, gave Adam some time to acclimate to his environment, to "settle in" to the reality of it. But there is much for the man to know, and there is much for him to do. Work awaits him and skills need to be developed.

The Recruit's New Reality

Soon enough, God begins to train Adam for his mission, his duties and his responsibilities. Adam needs to be trained for more as well. Remember, St. Michael and the angels hurled

Satan and his minions down to the earth (see Revelation 12:9). The potential for danger exists in the garden. Satan (Lucifer, once the Angel of Light) poses a threat to Adam and all God will entrust to him. Adam needs to become a good soldier, capable of discerning foe from friend, at the ready to defend and protect, prepared to lay down his life in the service of mission.

And so God trains the man in the way he should go. He informs Adam of his mission, issues commands in relation to it, and sets the expectation that Adam will respond with obedience. Adam's tutelage is not unlike that of a young military recruit.

When a military enlistee reports for duty on his first day, he may be filled with thoughts of grandeur. He may see himself piloting an Air Force fighter plane, commanding a naval warship, or strategizing an army battle. But the realities of his early days in military training fall far short of these great expectations. While he may accomplish his dreams at some point in his military career, the first order of business is to move him from a wide-eyed recruit to a soldier capable of defending his nation. A new perspective of who he is and what he can do, as well as the skill sets necessary to live out his mission, must be instilled within him.

Like Adam, the recruit may drink in the environment that surrounds him. Yet he soon discovers that his duties begin with three main areas of instruction:

1. First, he must *pay attention to detail.*

2. Second, he must *observe the chain of command.*

3. Lastly, he must *obey and follow through on lawful orders issued by those who outrank him.*

Instruction and commands begin on a very basic level. The recruit will learn that socks are to be folded *exactly* in half; when making his bunk, *perfect* hospital corners are expected, bed sheets folded back *precisely* six inches, catch-edge face down; commands will be followed *exactly*, without delay, and definitely with no lip.

Early on, the rules, regulations, and orders may seem superfluous, even silly. But they serve a higher purpose: They are structured to help the young recruit discover and unlock the great potential within him and the importance of those three foundational principles. What to him may seem like a small mistake is treated like a catastrophe of monumental proportions.

Why the fuss over seemingly insignificant things? Because failure by a solider in any of the three crucial areas—attention to detail, observance of the chain of command, obedience to and follow-through on all direct orders—can bring about defeat, destruction, and death for him, his comrades, and potentially the entirety of his nation. Nothing is a small matter in military training, because when engaged in combat, a seemingly insignificant thing can save the day or bring devastating, horrific consequences.

GOD'S COMMAND

God began Adam's training with a direct command that involves all three fundamental principles of training:

> The Lord God took the man and put him in the garden of
> Eden to till it and keep it. And the Lord God commanded
> the man, saying, "You may freely eat of every tree of the
> garden; but of the tree of the knowledge of good and evil
> you shall not eat, for in the day that you eat of it you shall
> die." (Genesis 2:15–17)

"Till the garden," God told the man. With this divine
mandate, Adam becomes "commander" over the garden and
all that will go on in it. Its care and cultivation are now his
responsibility: Adam would provide for the garden; his labor
would continue its orderly development according to God's
original design. In this way, his efforts would be united to
the Almighty's, and he would participate in God's sovereign
creative action. In turn, the garden's produce would provide
for him.

As the young military recruit's attention to detail could
eventually enable him to save lives, Adam's attention to the
details of the garden would sustain his life and the lives of
others. God was training him for increased responsibilities,
incorporating him into God's own role as provider.

Scripture tells us that there was more to Adam's responsibility for the garden. He was also to "keep" the garden. The
use of the word *keep* is interesting. The transliterated Hebrew
word *shamar* means "to guard, protect, and defend."[2] Adam
was to keep the garden secure and safe. But safe from what
or whom?

Perhaps Adam wondered at that question as he looked
around the garden, plucked a particularly juicy piece of fruit

from one of the trees, and bit into that fruit. Could it be the creatures that occupied the garden with him that would threaten it? Was there a predator yet unseen or an interloper yet to come that could disturb the sweet repose of this paradise? He did not know, but he knew he was called to be its defender and protector.

With the next command Adam received, God revealed the tactical knowledge necessary to maintain the garden's safety and Adam's as well. That command came from the heart of a loving Father who willed the best for His son: "You may freely eat of every tree of the garden, but of the tree of the knowledge of good and evil you shall not eat, for the day that you eat of it you shall die" (Genesis 2:17).

Surely Adam grasped the weight of this command! It resonates with God's sovereign authority and infinite love. He wished to protect His son, and the command He issued was meant to warn Adam of the grave consequence he would experience if he ate from the tree of the knowledge of good and evil. Failure to abide by this command meant he would die.

And herein lies Adam's test. Given the gift of free will, like the angels, he could choose for or against God. He could remain in God's perfect will and thereby enjoy all that is good, holy, and pure. Or he could choose against the commands of God and bring upon himself and his progeny the deleterious consequences of rejecting God and the infinitude of blessing God bestows.

The choice was his. Were his loyalty to God to be tested, would he obey God's command? Would he remain steadfast and fulfill his mission to "till" and "keep" the garden? Would he reflect God as provider and nurture all God entrusted to him? Would he reflect God's role as protector and safeguard what was entrusted to him? Would he be faithful to God and, by participating in God's divine authority and leadership, take benevolent dominion over creation? What would Adam do?

Time would tell.

AND THEN THERE WAS EVE

St. John Paul II tells us that, though Adam was created in the image and likeness of God, and though he had communion with God, he was in a profound state of loneliness. He was not God, nor was he a god. He dwelt in the garden with other creatures, but they were not like him, and he was not like them. The saint calls this dilemma "the original solitude."[3]

It is from Genesis 2 that St. John Paul's insight and theological wisdom derive. In verse 2:18, God says, "It is not good that the man should be alone; I will make a helper fit for him." The passage goes on to tell us that God's creation of the animals, the birds, and all other creatures was ordered to this end. But they were not the end themselves. Though Adam names the creatures, still none of them is a "helper fit for him." His loneliness remains profound and pervasive. Nothing in the garden, beautiful though it is, reflects to him the reality of who he is.

Of all that has been created, only Adam is made in the image and likeness of the Triune God, a communion of three divine Persons who give of themselves to each other in a self-donating communion of love. It is intrinsic to Adam's nature to know this same experience of love, but there is no being like himself, created with both a body and an immortal soul. No other incarnate being has a spiritual dimension. And without such a being to whom Adam can relate, he remains incomplete and unfulfilled, not knowing who he is. He is in the midst of an existential dilemma, the primordial identity crisis.

> So the Lord God caused a deep sleep to fall upon the man, and while he slept took one of his ribs and closed up its place with flesh; and the rib which the Lord God had taken from the man He made into a woman and brought her to the man. Then the man said,
>
> "This at last is bone of my bones
> and flesh of my flesh;
> she shall be called Woman,
> because she was taken out of Man."
>
> Therefore a man leaves his father and his mother and cleaves to his wife, and they become one flesh. (Genesis 2:21–24)

Imagine Adam's utter joy as he rouses from his sleep and beholds this glorious creature who stands before him! Like Adam, she is created in the image and likeness of God, beautiful in form and countenance, luminous with grace, a masterpiece of divine design. She has issued from Adam's side; she is part of him, and he is part of her.

St. John Paul II tells us that Adam and Eve saw each other as God saw them. In other words, they had his vision when gazing upon each other. As such, each saw the whole reality of his or her beloved. The pope wrote,

> Seeing each other, as if through the mystery of creation, man and woman see each other even more fully and distinctly than through the sense of sight itself.... They see and know each other with all the peace of the interior gaze, which creates precisely the fullness of the intimacy of persons.[4]

Adam looked at this one whom God presented to him, and something new and wonderful awakened within him. The woman touched the very core of his being. Gazing at her, he saw the essence of who he was—a discovery that can only be realized, says St. John Paul II, "by existing 'for someone.'"[5]

Eve was bone of his bones and flesh of his flesh! She completed him, and he found himself in her! His ecstatic "at last" only begins to express the deep longing he has known and his deep joy that it has been met.

But there is more. In the image and likeness of God, the man seeks to make a total gift of himself to the woman. And as Adam is a corporeal being, his gift comes by way of his body. He will be "one flesh" with Eve. And this coming together in an action of reciprocal gifting will lead to the fulfillment of the primordial command God issued to them as man and woman: "Be fruitful and multiply. Fill the earth and subdue it" (Genesis 1:28).

With this divine mandate, Adam's mission is no longer a singular enterprise. His mission is now a joint mission with the woman. Adam's masculine charisms take on a new significance.

MISSION EXPANDED

Adam exercises leadership by naming this new creature "Woman" and later Eve (Genesis 2:23; 3:20), just as he had named all the creatures entrusted to him. But Adam knows his duty toward her exceeds this one demonstration of masculine authority. He is to provide for her and protect her, and part of that protection is to train her as God trained him.

So perhaps Adam began as God began—with a trip through the garden. "What will Woman think of it all?" Adam may have mused as the couple set off. "Will she delight in the showy colors of the birds in the air?" "How will she respond to the rhinoceros, the giraffe, and the orangutan, the gazelle and lion and bear?" he may have wondered. "What will be her favorite flower: the fragrant rose or the sunny chamomile or the graceful iris?"

"Oh, and what fruit or berry will she like the best? Maybe the cherry or the pomegranate or the delicious apricot?" Perhaps a smile played at the corners of his lips as he anticipated her reactions.

Adam also had to point out to Eve the tree of the knowledge of good and evil. He had to be certain she understood God's command in reference to it. Perhaps he placed a protective arm about her as he recalled the awful consequence of eating its fruit.

Yes, Adam was her man, and she was his woman. He was to lead her, provide for her, and protect her. Perhaps a new sense of purpose, determination, and dignity laid hold of him as he escorted her through the garden.

With the creation of his new bride, Adam's mission expanded. His duties and responsibilities took on a deeper value and a deeper meaning. Woman, the apex of God's creation, was not like the other creatures. She was like himself: a person with a body and an immortal soul, created in the image and likeness of God. She was endowed with intellect, self-awareness, and free will.

Woman is to be at man's side in the enterprise of life. She is to assist him in the guarding, safekeeping, and nurturing of the garden. Like Adam, she must be a fit and able steward, a soldier of sorts, in keeping with her inherent feminine dignity and charisms. Adam is correct in this assessment. God's own language speaks to it. It's all tied up in the word *helpmate*.

Deacon Harold Burke-Sivers, in his book *Behold the Man: A Catholic Vision of Male Spirituality*, gives us a greater understanding of the relationship God intended for Adam and Eve when He created her from Adam's side as his "helpmate."

> The Hebrew word for "helpmate" is *ezer kenegdo*. The root of the word *ezer* means "power" and "strength." Combined with *kenegdo* ("opposite to" or "corresponding to"), the phrase was often used to denote one who stands opposite or parallel to the other who surrounds, protects, aids, helps, and supports, especially in battle. Woman is not created to be a maid or a servant to her husband— to make meals, do the laundry, and clean the house. God created woman in the same original solitude as the man (she is also superior to all of God's creatures, is self-aware, and can know God), but she possesses her own unique and

special gifts from God that complete and perfect the gifts of the man. They are to battle sin and death—together.[6]

Bible commentator Matthew Henry put it this way:

> The woman was made of a rib out of the side of Adam; not made out of his head to rule over him, nor out of his feet to be trampled upon by him, but out of his side to be equal with him, under his arm to be protected, and near his heart to be beloved.[7]

God took the woman from Adam's side to show her equality with him. She carries an authority as great as his but different from his.[8] Man and woman complete each other and together image the Trinitarian life. He is her protector, and she is his inspiration.

This was God's intention, His perfect will. But would it be fulfilled? The answer to that question lay within the free will of the man and the woman. What would they do? And, more importantly, what would God do? The answers to these questions are in our next chapter.

A Rosary Story
A Mother's Prayer
MIKE AQUILINA

It was probably as a zygote that I grew familiar with the Rosary. This prayer was a constant with my mom. She often had her beads in her hand or her pocket. She worked her Rosary while she worked the household. So if I'm to speak about the Rosary, I have to begin with my mother, who taught me whatever I know about Marian devotion.

My mom, quite conveniently, was named Mary. And she had very Marian beginnings. Mom was born in 1916 and grew up in the decades immediately after the Marian apparitions at Fatima, Portugal—when even the *New York Times* talked about the Rosary on its front pages. Twice a year, the men of our little ethnic parish near Scranton, Pennsylvania, would lift a large statue of the Blessed Virgin onto their shoulders and carry it through the streets. They were accompanied by a marching band and fireworks.

The wider culture eventually confirmed the Marian piety we had inherited from our Sicilian ancestors. If you tuned in on the radio, you could listen to Fr. Patrick Peyton promoting the Rosary. A few years later, Bishop Fulton Sheen was preaching the same message on TV. That piety took flesh in our family. Mom gave three of my sisters Marian names: Assunta (for the Assumption), Rosaria, and Mary.

My mother's faith was deeply Christ-centered. Her love for Our Lord grew as she spent time meditating on the mysteries of his life in the company of his mother. From Mom I learned that Marian devotion was not a distraction from Jesus but rather a sharing in all the things "his mother kept...in her heart" (Luke 2:51).

Mom prayed for each of her seven children through the trials and crises of childhood, adolescence, and adulthood. When her nest was finally empty, I'll bet she even got to pray five decades of the Rosary in one sitting—or one kneeling. Prayer was her most effective way of continuing to mother us. I believe it's my mother's faith—a Mediterranean peasant faith—that disposed me to study the Scriptures and the early Church Fathers.

When Mom was eighty-five, she underwent major surgery, then suffered a stroke. The immediate effects of the stroke were devastating. Mom recognized me only intermittently, which was far more difficult for me than I ever could have predicted. Till that moment (I was thirty-nine), I was sure I was the son at the center of her solar system.

My sisters made sure Mom had her Rosary with her at all times. Though she had lost much, she still knew how to move her fingers along the beads and say the basic prayers of the Catholic faith—the Our Father, Hail Mary, and Glory Be. That action had burned neural pathways that were deep and ineradicable. These proved to be the pathways to her healing. Her Rosary was the lifeline that pulled her back to health.

Mom continued praying the Rosary till her death at ninety-five. My last conversation with her was about the rich meaning of the phrase *gratia plena*, "full of grace," the title the angel Gabriel gave Mary in the Gospel of

St. Luke (Luke 1:28). How I love to pray, "Hail Mary, full of grace..."

Thanks, Mom. And thank you, Blessed Mother!

Mike Aquilina is the author of many books, including Angels of God, Understanding the Mass, *and* Keeping Mary Close.

Chapter Five

All Was Well Until It Wasn't

THE FALL OF MAN AND GOD'S AMAZING PROVISION

The knot of Eve's disobedience was loosed
by the obedience of Mary.
For what the virgin Eve had bound fast through
unbelief, this did the Virgin Mary set free
through faith. [1]

—ST. IRENAEUS

Scripture gives us no hint as to how long the idyllic peace of the garden existed. We only know that after God created Adam and the woman, He appraised His work, found everything "very good," and then rested on the seventh day (Genesis 1:31; 2:2). Because a "day" in biblical terms can be a thousand years (see Psalm 90:4), Adam and his bride may have enjoyed the garden's tranquility for some time. We don't know. What we do know is that their state of innocence didn't last.

Remember that St. Michael and the angels hurled Satan and his troops down to the earth (see Revelation 12:7–9), the physical environment God created for the persons who bore His image and likeness. It would be here that the battle begun in the heavenlies would continue until the end of time. Upon this plane, the devil would seek vengeance for the woman of the vision and her offspring. However, though he was privy to God's plan, Satan was not privy to God's timing.

We might picture the scene, another lovely day in Eden. The birds are singing, the water is tinkling, the cool breeze of late afternoon softly rustles the leaves of the trees. The woman is in the middle of the garden. Adam might be with her, but there is no definitive teaching on this. Some translations of Sacred Scripture suggest he was; others do not.[2]

If Adam was with his wife, perhaps he was distracted and didn't notice that she had become attracted to a "wild creature that the Lord God had made" (Genesis 3:1). Or perhaps he just stood there and watched the event unfold. We don't know, but we do know that in some way, he abdicated his responsibility to the woman. He left her vulnerable.

The wily creature captivated the woman. The serpent was frighteningly different from anything else in the garden, truly awful to behold. And yet something in its perverse appearance was alluring. The serpent beguiled the woman; its seduction held her fast.

The Bitter Fruit of Consequence

What was this creature and from whence did it come? The Hebrew transliteration for its name gives us the answer, *nachash*. It is translated as "serpent" or "dragon." Recall chapter 12 of the book of Revelation. St. John's vision shows the true nature of this creature. There, Satan is described as "a great red dragon, with seven heads and ten horns, and seven diadems upon his heads" (12:3). The dragon's name is "Devil and Satan, the deceiver of the whole world" (12:9). It is the fallen angel Lucifer, who fell from heaven at the sword of St. Michael and his angels (see Isaiah 14:12–15; Luke 10:18).

The serpent is interested in only one thing: taking out the masterpiece of God's creation—man, both male and female. This disobedient instigator of sedition and rebellion has come out of the shadows of darkness and entered the garden. And his sole intent is to engage, seduce, and destroy the pinnacle of the created order, the creatures made in God's own image and likeness. His goal is to foil God's perfect will.

It is the woman Satan has in his crosshairs. His hatred toward her is intense. Saint Maximilian Kolbe gives us a possible reason why. His explanation is found in the draft of the book he was writing on the Mother of God prior to his martyrdom. After recalling the events of Revelation 12, and Satan's prideful rebellion against the Woman who would be his Queen, the Saint writes, "In the Garden of Eden, Satan saw a being like the One who was the object of his anger. He cannot reach God, he cannot reach her [Mary], but pours out his hatred onto her future mother, on the first mother of mankind [Eve]."[3]

And so, at the sight of Eve in the garden, his fury builds. It is a daughter of hers that will bear the "male child who will rule all of the nations with a rod of iron" (Revelation 12:5). Satan bristles at the thought, and a wave of vitriol and contempt boil up in him. He has but one goal in mind – destroy this woman in the garden. And so, masking his fury, he cunningly entices the woman to the tree of the knowledge of good and evil to employ his destructive plan.

His strategy is threefold: (1) He will engage the woman by falsifying God's command about this tree; (2) he will raise suspicions and doubts in her mind about God's good will; (3) he will portray God as her enemy. "It's a brilliant plan," he thinks to himself, "shrewdly engineered and calibrated. It will work." He snarls with satisfaction. And the rest, as they say, is history:

> He said to the woman, "Did God say, 'You shall not eat of any tree of the garden?'" And the woman said to the serpent, "We may eat of the fruit of the trees of the garden; but God said, 'You shall not eat of the fruit of the tree in the midst of the garden, neither shall you touch it, lest you die.'" But the serpent said to the woman, "You will not die. For God knows that when you eat of it your eyes will be opened, and you will be like God, knowing good and evil." So when the woman saw that the tree was good for food, and that it was a delight to the eyes, and that the tree was to be desired to make one wise, she took of its fruit and ate; and she also gave some to her husband, and

he ate. Then the eyes of both were opened, and they knew that they were naked; and they sewed fig leaves together and made themselves aprons. (Genesis 3:1–7)

This is perhaps one of the key passages in Sacred Scripture. In fact, one might make the case that it is the hinge upon which Sacred Scripture swings. Everything that follows is because of this one disobedient act. Salvation history develops from here. The passage bears a deeper look.

Satan's strategy was to entice the woman. His hatred for her was reason enough to take her down, but the man was his ultimate target, and the devil was confident that the woman was the means of getting to him. Why was the man the prize to be won? The answer is simply this: If evil, death, and destruction were to enter the world, he would need to fail the test God put in place. He would need to disobey God's direct command.

Recall that it was to Adam that God gave dominion over the whole of the garden. It was to him that God issued the order to "till" and "keep" it, thereby commanding Adam to cultivate and guard the garden. God also commanded him, "You shall not eat of the fruit of the tree of the knowledge of good and evil, lest you die." And God entrusted to Adam the protection and provision of the apex of his creation, woman. All of God's created order was Adam's duty and responsibility.

In military terms, Adam was the commanding officer charged by God. "The buck stopped" with him. He had authority over creation. And so the *consequences* of sin began when he disobeyed.

This reality becomes evident in verse seven of the passage just quoted. Note that no consequence immediately occurred when Eve ate the fruit. All began to devolve when Adam ate it. With his action, the consequences of sin began and the original innocence was lost. That was when "the eyes of both of them were opened, and they knew they were naked."

We'll look at this passage in more detail a little later on, but for now, let's ask the question, why was the woman the means of getting to the man?

INTRINSIC REALITIES: THE NATURE OF MAN AND WOMAN

Recall the words that Adam speaks when he beholds the woman for the first time. He calls her "bone of my bones and flesh of my flesh." As was previously stated, these words communicate that Adam "found" himself in the woman. Gertrud von le Fort, in her book *The Eternal Woman*, written in 1934, interprets the significance of woman according to her *symbolic* aspect.

In philosophical terms, a *sign* or *symbol* points to the metaphysical reality of something. Metaphysics, as it is used in philosophy, has to do with the fundamental nature of reality and being, the essential nature of things, so to speak. Gertrud von le Fort defines symbols as "signs or images through which ultimate metaphysical realities and modes of being are apprehended...by way of a likeness.... [They] are therefore the language of an invisible reality becoming articulate in the realm of the visible."[4] In other words, we get to know or understand the invisible realities via the visible realities.

Von le Fort continues, "This concept of the symbol springs from the conviction that in all beings and things there is an intelligent order that, through these very beings and things, reveals itself as a divine order by means of the language of its symbols."[5]

What then is the sign or symbol of the woman? To what intrinsic reality might she point? Von le Fort tells us, "From the point of view of her symbol, woman has a special filiation with the religious sphere...and this, as belonging to the symbol, has been in a special measure entrusted to the woman."[6] In some way, the mystery of woman, "the metaphysical countenance of woman," as von le Fort calls it, takes the eyes upward to the mysteries of God and inward to the soul of the human person.

We might say then that, metaphysically, woman is the sign of that which is hidden, mysterious, holy, sacred.[7] Even the physiology of woman indicates as much. Her reproductive organs are hidden in the interior of her being and shrouded in veils. In Sacred Scripture, that which is holy is always covered and concealed, its purity guarded that it might not be profaned.[8] The holy is set apart and reverenced, for its reference is transcendent and belongs to the heavenlies.

Consider this: It is within the sacred vessel of woman's womb that God will infuse an immortal soul into the union of sperm and egg to create an unrepeatable human person, made in His image and likeness, who will exist for all eternity. This remarkable beginning is in itself a sign. It signifies God's holy entrustment of the human person to the woman. The babe's life on every level will come from her being: She will suckle this one, nourish this one, reveal identity to this one, and lead this one to the fullness of life in God. Indeed, woman shares uniquely in the majesty and sacredness of the Almighty and in His plan of salvation.

We might think of woman's beginning as an additional indication of her metaphysical reality. Unlike the man, who was formed from the clay of the earth, woman is deep coming from deep. She is fashioned from an interior part of the man. Taken from his depths, she references and reveals to him the innermost reality of who he is. She makes his interior exterior and holds it high for him to see.

There is yet another aspect to the significance of woman's origin. She is molded from Adam's rib, his bone. It is the skeleton that gives shape and stature to the human form. Woman will lift up her man in the emotional and spiritual realm. She will help him to be upstanding in thought and word and deed, encouraging his rise to full stature and his reach for the ultimate good, who is God himself.

Hence we hear Adam's cry and acknowledgment that he knows himself in beholding her. The woman points him upward to his metaphysical reality and inspires him to attain it and live it. [9] This is Eve's mission toward Adam: to be his inspiration and likewise to inspire human civilization. Her influence, effect, and power—her feminine authority—rest on this principle: She is chosen by God to bring to fulfillment, and ultimate potential, the life entrusted to her by virtue of her very nature, her feminine reality. [10]

The sacrifice of Adam's rib for woman's creation has its own significance and speaks to his mission as man. It defines him as a participant in God's own fatherhood, from which all creation flows. Woman's issuing from him signifies that he references the Almighty, the First Cause.[11] It connotes his call to be Godlike in his care of woman: to cherish she who comes forth from him and to guard her, to sacrifice for her, to "slay dragons" for her, to lay down his life for her if called. He is to be her protector, provider, and leader and to be the same for all those born as the fruit of their union. This is the mark of his masculinity, the mark of his fatherhood, the mark of his Godlikeness.

And as with woman, the man's physiology speaks to this divine duty. While the woman's reproductive organs are hidden away in her body, indicating her call to the nurturance of life inside the womb and out, the man's reproductive system speaks to the exterior call and mission that is his. God has commanded him to take dominion over the created order—to conquer it, develop it, maintain it, and sustain it for the safety and provision of those entrusted to him. His masculine authority is designed to bring order, stability, and fruitfulness to the exterior world in service to those who are his by way of entrustment. This is his very nature, his masculine reality.

The complementarity between man and woman, which comes by way of the lived expression of their individual authorities, is a dynamic of gift-to-gift through which comes human flourishing—and the flourishing of all creation, for that matter. This is what Satan observed, and this is what he was intent on destroying.

WHAT WAS THE DEVIL THINKING?

Though he is not omniscient, the Evil One is nonetheless an acutely aware and intelligent observer. His reasoning skills, coupled with his intuitive acumen, make him a formidable foe. Remember, before the heavenly rebellion, his name was Lucifer, which means "light bearer" or "angel of light." He was a seraphic angel and the brightest of the choir.

The devil's observation skills were at the ready in the garden. He more than noticed the interaction between Adam and Eve. He may have overheard Adam's exclamation when he beheld the woman for the first time: "This at last is bone of my bones and flesh of my flesh" (Genesis 2:23).

The devil rightly determines that Eve exerts an influence, effect, and power over Adam. He has watched Adam come to self-knowledge and self-possession through her inspiration and guidance. He determines that the man is "at home" when with her, and the very sight of her breathes life into the man, emboldening his masculine charisms. She is his North Star, guiding him toward the fulfillment of his male authority.

In complete possession of his masculine identity, the source of which is God himself, Adam is daunting prey. The full weight of his authority as protector may yield the unpleasant consequence of a foiled plan. And once discovered, Satan may never have the opportunity again. "No," he determines, "confronting the man is not a good option."

But the woman is another matter completely. Not only has Satan observed the way she inspires Adam, but he has also noticed that her feminine authority leads her to nurture the whole of creation in a life-giving way. As she engages Adam, she also engages the world around her. And this could well be exploited.

Satan deduces that Eve is the lynchpin to his diabolical scheme. If he gets Eve, he will get Adam. So he puts his plan in play, and all hell breaks loose.

AFTER THE FALL

Once original sin entered the world, "the eyes of both [the man and woman] were opened, and they knew that they were naked" (Genesis 3:7). This passage gives us insight and understanding into the reality of sin. As the *Catechism of the Catholic Church* tells us, all sin ruptures man's communion with God (*CCC*, 1440), wounds his nature (*CCC*, 1872), and severs human solidarity (*CCC*, 1872). Put simply, sin dis-integrates.

Recall that Adam and Eve were created in the image and likeness of God. They were full of grace, and their free will was conformed to God's will. Thus, they were able to freely receive God's love and freely give their love to Him in return. The fruit of this loving union was peace. Man was at peace in God, man was at peace in himself, and man's interior peace flowed over into his relationship with the rest of the created world. Spiritual writers refer to this supernatural state of peace as the "triple harmony." This was the peace Adam and the woman knew in the garden.

But after Adam partakes of the fruit, he and the woman begin to lose everything, starting with their innocence. "They knew that they were naked; and they sewed fig leaves together

and made themselves aprons" (Genesis 3:7). Their relationship—once pure and chaste, unencumbered by sin—is now
compromised by the passion of lust. Adam's body betrays his
desire, and Eve feels the sting of objectification. The "one-
fleshedness" of their union is strained, and their solidarity is
severed. To hide their shame, they cover themselves.

The fracture extends beyond their interpersonal dynamic.
Their sin rends their relationship with God as well. When the
Lord approaches, Adam and Eve retreat to the bushes to hide.
Scripture says that when "God called out to the man," he
responded, "I heard the sound of thee in the garden, and
I was afraid because I was naked" (Genesis 3:10). Fear, the
noxious fruit of disobedience, has found root in the man. It
immediately produces additional bad fruit: When God questions Adam about their actions, Adam indirectly blames God
and then Eve; Eve, then, blames the serpent (vv. 11–13).

Recall the *Catechism*'s assertion that sin "wounds man's
nature" (*CCC*, 1872). Recall also that, when speaking of
the nature of something, we are talking about its ontolog-
ical reality, its essence. We have seen that the essence of man
speaks to the reality of his masculine authority and the way it
is lived out. Man is uniquely called to tame the world, make it
produce, and navigate or lead others through it. By protecting
and providing for those entrusted to him, he makes a way for
others to reach their fulfillment and ultimate potential, which
is the likeness of God.

It is for this reason that God calls out to the man in the
garden and not the woman. God addresses him first about the
actions that have taken place. The garden, and everything in
it, is Adam's masculine domain, his territory.

Likewise, we have seen how the woman's metaphysical reality defines who she is. Human life is entrusted to her interior, and her call is not only to bear this life and nurture this life in the physical sense but also to tend to its spiritual dimension. She is to point others to the sacred. Just as egg and sperm meet within her, making her biological mother, so too she is called to gestate and nurture unto life the hearts and souls of those entrusted to her, making her their spiritual mother. Through her feminine authority, she encourages, affirms, inspires, and brings to full potential the children—physical and spiritual—placed in her maternal care. Simply put, she is to assist them in the achievement of their God-likeness through union with Him.

Unscathed by sin prior to the fall, Adam and Eve lived the fullness of their authority, masculine and feminine. But once they sinned, their natures were wounded, and they acted contrary to their metaphysical reality. Rather than leading her man to godly heights, Eve leads him to perdition. Adam, having left the woman unprotected, further abdicates his masculine authority when he blames her for his actions. And she then blames the serpent.

Man's nature has been wounded by sin. Dis-integration has taken place. Can healing and restoration come?

GOD'S PROMISE: THE PROTO-EVANGELIUM

The answer to this question comes in the context of the penalties each of the actors in this drama will experience. God is both merciful and just. Perhaps had Adam and Eve repented of their sin rather than justifying it, things may have turned out differently. But they did not seek God's mercy. And so it is in justice that God tells Adam and Eve their sin merits stiff punishment.

Eve will bring forth her children in pain, but her urge will be for her husband, who will "rule over her." While up until now the earth has produced fruit and grain with little of Adam's effort, it will now yield thorn and thistle instead, and great will be the labor Adam will expend to make it produce. Worst of all, made out of the dust of the ground, Adam and his progeny will return to it through death. Their lives will end (see Genesis 3:16–19).

All of this sounds like cause for great despair, but in the penalty meted out to the serpent, we find hope and cause for rejoicing. It comes just before Adam and Eve become aware of their fate and is known as the Proto-Evangelium, the "first Gospel" or the "first good news." It is the whole of salvation history in a nutshell:

> I will put enmity between you and the woman,
> and between your seed and her seed;
> he shall bruise your head,
> and you shall bruise his heel. (Genesis 3:15)

Here God tells the serpent that it will be cursed among the animals, crawl on its belly, and eat dust all the days of its life.[12] This is good news indeed! While man is in the midst of his depravity, God is making provision for him. Another day is coming. And this day will see the triumph of the woman and "her seed." And their triumph will bring freedom and abundant life to all of humanity and creation.

So who is *this* woman, and who is her seed? And how will they triumph?

It has been the consistent teaching of the Catholic Church that the woman of the Proto-Evangelium is the Blessed Virgin Mary, and the seed is Jesus Christ, the Son of God, who will be born of her in the fullness of time (see Galatians 4:4). Mary is the New Eve, and her Son, Jesus Christ, is the New Adam. Unlike the pair who led man to perdition, this holy pair will lead mankind to salvation. Together the victory will be theirs by virtue of their masculine and feminine authority, lived out in union with God's perfect will.

Mary's *fiat mihi*, "Let it be done to me" (Luke 1:38), is her active surrender to the fertile action of the Holy Spirit. It will be the means by which the Son of God enters into time. As her *yes* gives way to Jesus's physical birth, so will her continued *fiat* birth her Son into His mission. She will inspire Him in the way He should go and stand with Him in His "hour," His Passion and death. She will be his *ezer kenegdo*, His "helpmate," and He will win the day!

Although the serpent will mount an offensive against the Redeemer, striking at his heel, the Redeemer will crush the serpent's head, dealing him a mortal blow. That blow will come by way of the ultimate sacrifice: Jesus will lay down His life for those entrusted to Him, thereby meriting restoration of the wounded nature of man. What is more, the authority of the New Adam and of the New Eve will endure until the end of time. Their authority is decisive in the war the devil wages against the woman and her seed (see Revelation 12:17).

Through her maternal beatitude, Mary draws her spiritual children to the wellspring of grace that flows from her

Son's redemptive act. That grace nourishes, fortifies, and strengthens Christians. As the Fathers of the Second Vatican Council state, "By her maternal charity, she cares for the brethren of her Son, who still journey on earth surrounded by dangers and [difficulties], until they are led into the happiness of their true home."[13]

Such has been the work of the Blessed Virgin Mary from the nascent Church in Palestine unto the present day, and such will be her work until the end of time. As St. Louis de Montfort states in his treatise *True Devotion to Mary*, "It was through Mary that the salvation of the world was begun, and it is through Mary that it must be consummated."[14]

Mary's maternal care comes by way of her role as Mediatrix of grace—grace that flows from the superabundant merits of Christ (see *CCC*, 964). The Church throughout the ages has affirmed this doctrine of Mary, invoking her under the titles of Advocate, Helper, Benefactress, and Mediatrix (*CCC*, 969).[15] St. Louis de Montfort states it eloquently:

> God the Son has communicated to His Mother all that He acquired by His life and His death, His infinite merits and His admirable virtues; and He has made her the treasurer of all that His Father gave Him for His inheritance. It is by her that He applies His merits to His members, and that He communicates His virtues, and distributes His graces. She is His mysterious canal; she is His aqueduct, through which He makes His mercies flow gently and abundantly.[16]

According to de Montfort, Mary's maternal intercession will be especially pronounced in the latter days,[17] when the wiles of the Evil One will be particularly virulent:

Mary must be terrible to the devil and his crew, as an army ranged in battle, principally in these latter times, because the devil, knowing that he has but little time, and now less than ever, to destroy souls, will every day redouble his efforts and his combats. He will presently raise up cruel persecutions and will put terrible snares before the faithful servants and true children of Mary, whom it gives him more trouble to conquer than it does to conquer others.[18]

Indeed, the historic record shows that time and again, at critical moments in the world of man, Mary has intervened on behalf of the brethren of Christ. She has revealed the "infernal plots" and scattered the "diabolical councils" of the Evil One and has led her children to safety and wellbeing.[19] In fact, as we have seen, through her maternal intercession, she has conquered heretics, held invaders at bay, prevented catastrophes, and stopped communist aggression.

And it seems that, since the thirteenth century, time and again Our Lady's weapon of choice has been the Holy Rosary. Through this mighty prayer, countless miracles have been obtained, and a host of victories have been won. In this day and time, besieged as we are by the myriad tricks, tactics, and machinations of evil, we would do well to consider Mary's maternal protection by way of this ancient devotion.

In our next chapter, we will discover how we can enter this prayer and devotional practice more deeply to reap abundant blessings for ourselves and for others.

A Rosary Story

My Wonderful Rosary

DONNA-MARIE COOPER O'BOYLE

Growing up Catholic, I was accustomed to seeing Rosary beads at home and at my grandmother's house. Large Rosary beads also hung on the black habits of the sisters who taught me at my elementary school and whom I admired. Particularly etched on my heart are the times when my mother drew her children together in our home before a small flickering candle in blue glass, set before a statue of the Blessed Mother. Perhaps unknowingly but nonetheless, my mother set a very powerful example for her eight children by teaching us the ancient prayer of the Rosary.

My path became crooked after I left home, yet whenever I experienced something harrowing or traumatic, my heart was drawn to prayer and especially to Mother Mary. One time I was held captive by a man with a machine gun (I detail this in my memoir, *The Kiss of Jesus*), and a Rosary suddenly showed up! I believe that Mother Mary was watching over me.

Later on, when I became a wife and mother, I often turned to the beautiful prayer of the Rosary. Many a night I nursed my babies and rocked them back to sleep to this soothing prayer. I taught the Rosary to my children as well. We prayed for those in need, at home and also when traveling in the car, which I found to be a perfect time to pray at least a decade together. Throughout the years of mothering my brood of five, I often resorted to my ten fingertips to count my Hail Marys when the task I was immersed in did not allow for holding the beads.

I have seen this blessed sacramental move people from fear to instant peace. One time I gave my Rosary beads to a frightened young woman on an airplane when we were going through violent turbulence. A non-Catholic mother once accepted the gift of my Rosary and held it each time she felt fearful. She said she didn't know what she would do without it.

I have no doubt that the Blessed Mother works powerfully through her Rosary and desires that we pray it faithfully each day.

Donna-Marie Cooper O'Boyle is an EWTN TV host and the award-winning author of over twenty books, including The Miraculous Medal: Stories, Prayers, and Devotions *and* The Kiss of Jesus: How Mother Teresa and the Saints Helped Me to Discover the Beauty of the Cross.

Chapter Six

Engaging the Battle

ENTERING THE POWER AND
MYSTERY OF THE ROSARY

The grave challenges confronting the world at
the start of this new Millennium lead us to think
that only an intervention from on high, capable of
guiding the hearts of those living in situations of
conflict and those governing the destinies of nations,
can give reason to hope for a brighter future.

—POPE JOHN PAUL II, *RVM*, 40

In his exquisite apostolic letter on the Rosary, *Rosarium
Virginis Mariae*, Pope John Paul II explains that the
Rosary continues to be a source of spiritual power for us
today, just as it was in centuries past.

The history of the Rosary shows how this prayer was used
in particular by the Dominicans at a difficult time for the

Church due to the spread of heresy. Today we are facing new challenges. Why should we not once more have recourse to the Rosary, with the same faith as those who have gone before us? The Rosary retains all its power and continues to be a valuable resource for every good evangelizer. (*RVM*, 17)

Thus the Holy Father reminds us of something another great pope, Pope Leo XIII, wrote:

Sometimes we have seen the fervor of piety grow cold in certain countries and the practice of reciting the *Rosary* decline. Then an astonishing thing happens; either by reason of some great public danger or under the pressure of some necessity, the recitation of the *Rosary* has been reestablished more than all other prayers.[1]

In our day and time, a reestablishment of the Rosary seems to be the most effective way to battle the enemy's forces invading our homes, our families, our communities, our country, and our culture. In chapter one, we saw a historic perspective of the Rosary's victories; we can have every confidence it will be victorious again. Why? Because, as St. John Paul II reminds us, it has *power*. From whence does this power come?

THE ROSARY: AT THE HEART OF CHRISTIAN LIFE

While we may be tempted to look at the Rosary and its devotional practice as a simple recitation of five decades of Hail Marys preceded by the Apostles' Creed and interspersed with Our Fathers and Glory Bes, this would be a myopic view of the magnitude and power of this great and holy prayer. In fact, in his apostolic letter on the Rosary, Pope John Paul II leads us to see that the prayer of the Rosary is capable of conforming us to Christ. What can this yield for us in light of the difficulties and trials we face personally and corporately as the people of God? Well, according to one spiritual writer, it can yield for us the very power of Christ!

Fr. Emil Neubert, a leading Mariologist of the twentieth century, gives us insight.[2] Like Pope John Paul II, Fr. Neubert was both a devotee of St. Louis de Montfort's *True Devotion* and a champion of the Rosary. In *Queen of Militants*, one of his many works on Our Lady, he exhorts his readers to have confidence in the battle, because they are *omnipotent with Christ*.[3] Here is one thrilling passage from a chapter appropriately named "How to Pray for the Combat":

> "Without me you can do nothing," [Christ] Himself told us.... To the feeling of your *powerlessness without Christ* you must join the conviction of your *omnipotence with Christ*. After affirming that nothing could be done without Him, He added: "He who abides in me, and I in him, he bears much fruit" (John 15:5). Like the Apostle Paul, you should feel that you can do all things in Him Who strengthens you (Philippians 4:13).[4]

The power to be victorious over the machinations of the Evil One, which assail us from all sides and affect us personally and corporately, comes via the abiding presence of Jesus Christ and our conformity to Him. How does the prayer of the Rosary bring us to this presence and conformity?

Pope John Paul II points to the Rosary's "full meaning." He tells us, "The Rosary, reclaimed in its full meaning, goes to the very heart of Christian life," in that it offers a "fruitful spiritual and educational opportunity for personal contemplation, the formation of the People of God, and the new evangelization" (*RVM*, 3).[5] In other words, the Rosary, *in its full meaning*, is a prayer of contemplation that forms the people of God according to the mind and heart of Christ. God's people in turn affect the whole world, through Him and in Him. This powerful and efficacious prayer is a path of transformation, a training ground for holiness that can lead us to full stature in Christ Jesus (see Ephesians 4:13) and the full realization of our God-given authority.

CONTEMPLATION: THE PATH TO HOLINESS AND TRANSFORMATION

Pope John Paul II tells us, "The Rosary should always be seen and experienced as a path of contemplation" (*RVM*, 38). The *Catechism of the Catholic Church* provides us with many insights regarding contemplative prayer and highlights many of its facets (see *CCC*, 2709–2719). But contemplative prayer is perhaps most beautifully described as "a *gaze* of faith, fixed on Jesus" (*CCC*, 2715).

Our gaze upon the Lord is a "renunciation of self," an act of receptivity, trust, and surrender. In the end, it is an act of humility and vulnerability to the love of God (see 2 Corinthians 3:18). But this gaze is not a one-way gaze. Jesus looks on us as well.

Jesus's gaze, the *Catechism* tells us, both purifies our heart and illumines the eyes of our heart. It "teaches us to see everything in the light of [Jesus's] truth and his compassion for all men." Additionally, contemplation "turns its gaze on the mysteries of the life of Christ," which yields an "interior knowledge of our Lord," helping us to love Him more deeply and follow Him more fervently (CCC, 2715).[6]

In his letter on the Rosary, John Paul II tells us that the "*incomparable model*" of the contemplation of Christ is Mary. His face "belongs" to her, having been shaped and formed within her womb. His face received from her "a human resemblance." This human resemblance, the pope tells us, "points to an even greater spiritual closeness" (*RVM*, 10).

Mary's eyes were turned upon Jesus from the moment she conceived Him by the power of the Holy Spirit at the Annunciation. Even then, she sensed his growing presence within her and pondered the joy of seeing his wee features at his birth. And John Paul II says, "Thereafter Mary's gaze, ever filled with adoration and wonder, would never leave him" (*RVM*, 10).[7]

In fact, the pope tells us, "Mary lived with her eyes fixed on Christ." She treasured His words and pondered them in her heart. The memories of Jesus were "impressed upon her heart" and were for her "the 'Rosary' which she recited uninterruptedly throughout her earthly life" (*RVM*, 11).

John Paul II concludes this paragraph with a poignant statement, the first part of which he emphasizes with italics:

Mary constantly sets before the faithful the "mysteries" of her Son, with the desire that the contemplation of those mysteries will release all their saving power. In the recitation of the Rosary, the Christian community enters into contact with the memories and the contemplative gaze of Mary. (*RVM*, 11)

Such a beautiful statement, and so insightful that it requires another look. How can pondering the mysteries through Mary's eyes lead us more deeply into the power and efficacy of the Rosary?

THE POWER OF REMEMBERING

Pope John Paul II raises two points about the power of remembering that may lead us more deeply into the power and efficacy of the Rosary: First, there is a connection between contemplating the mysteries of the life of Christ and their power being released. Second, when we pray the Rosary, we *are brought into contact with the memories of Mary's gaze.*

What does contemplating the mysteries of Jesus have to do with the release of their power? And how can we have *contact* with "the memories of Mary's contemplative gaze"?

It is all about the word *remembering*, as understood in the biblical sense. The Holy Father tells us that above all, Mary's contemplation was a *remembering*. In the biblical sense, "remembrance" is "*a making present* of the works brought about by God in the history of salvation" (*RVM*, 13, italics added). It is with this understanding of the word, for example, that Jesus tells the apostles at the Last Supper, "Do this in remembrance of me" (Luke 22:19).

As sacred mysteries, the events of God exist in the eternal moment: They take place in time and space but are not bound by time and space. The grace of these events is always available via the "remembering." Rather than a nostalgic gaze at the past, this type of gaze brings the full weight of the past into the present moment. John Paul II put it this way: "These events [of Christ's life] not only belong to 'yesterday'; *they are also part of the 'today' of salvation*" (*RVM*, 13).

Highlighting the preeminence of the liturgy and the grace that flows from it into all other devotions, the pope tells us that "to remember [what God accomplished centuries ago] in a spirit of faith and love is to be open to the grace which Christ won for us by the mysteries of his life, death and resurrection" (*RVM*, 13).

We have at least some sense of this from our own human remembrances. There are times when we simply gaze back at an event. We may remember when it happened, who was with us, and other pertinent details. But other memories reach deeply into our psyche. These memories come not only with those kinds of details but often with an emotional, if not visceral, response. For an instant, we feel transported back to the moment itself; we "relive" it, so to speak.

Now, what if that moment, in the fullness of its essence and reality, could become present in this new moment in time via the remembrance? It would not be a transporting from the present into the past but rather a transporting of the past into the present. This is the Jewish understanding of the word *zakar*, or "remembrance." It is a "making present again."

Scripture scholar Peter Toon puts it succinctly: It is "making present the past, so that it can be effective in the present."[8]

When we speak of the "mysteries of faith," these are not mysteries to be solved in detective-like fashion. Rather, they transcend or exceed our intellect. They are to be entered into and experienced, and they likewise are to penetrate our very being and bring about a change or transformation in us.

Mysteries of faith are inexhaustible in their scope, beatitude, and efficacy. Therefore, though they cannot be fully apprehended or quantified, their effects are recognizable and felt. And as many theologians and spiritual writers attest, the more a prayer or devotion expresses our adherence to the person of Jesus Christ and His salvific work or praise for the Blessed Trinity and the Incarnate Word, the more we are assimilated to these mysteries and are protected by them.[9]

Would not the Rosary then—focused as it is on the sacred mysteries of Christ's life, penetrating these mysteries with the gaze of Mary, invoking and praising the Trinity with each doxology—rank high among the most efficacious prayers and devotional practices? And would it not then provide a superlative degree of protection and offer a superlative grace of transformation? It is through such contemplation that the power and efficacy of the mysteries of Christ are released and made present to us.

ENTERING THE SCHOOL OF MARY

How could we possibly have *contact* with "the memories of Mary's contemplative gaze"? Pope John Paul II alludes to the answer in the introduction of his apostolic letter. He says that through the Rosary, we sit "at the school of Mary" and are led to "contemplate the beauty on the face of Christ and to experience the depths of his love." Through the Rosary, we "receive abundant grace, as though from the very hands of the Mother of the Redeemer" (*RVM*, 1). The Rosary "mystically transports us to Mary's side," he says, enabling her to train us and to mold us with the same care she showed Jesus, "until Christ is 'fully formed' in us" (*RVM*, 15; see Galatians 4:19).[10]

We can better understand this truth in light of our discussion on remembrance. By praying the Rosary and consciously calling to mind in faith the mysteries of the life of Christ, the grace of those mysteries becomes present to us and efficacious for us. Mary, our spiritual mother who always leads us to her Son, mystically takes us into her "gaze" of those mysteries, to behold the face of Christ with her. Mary, in her maternal beatitude, shows us how to obtain from the Holy Spirit the graces we need. As the incarnate life of the Word was nurtured within Mary's womb, so is our spiritual life nurtured within her Immaculate Heart. In this sacred place, we become "*an icon of Christian contemplation*" (*RVM*, 9), like Peter, James, and John at the moment of Jesus's transfiguration.

This process of "gazing" with Mary yields abundant fruit. We become conformed to Christ. St. Paul's stunning words apply to us: "Beholding the glory of the Lord, [we] are being changed into his likeness, from one degree of glory to another; for this comes from the Lord who is the Spirit" (2 Corinthians

3:18). Simply put, we become transformed. We become like the one we are beholding (see *RVM*, 9).

Author Dr. Anthony Lilles tells us, "When we gaze into the eyes of Christ with the eyes of our heart, we begin to see things as they truly are. Under His gaze of love our prayer begins to resonate with the will of the Father."[11]

"The Rosary," says John Paul II, "helps us to be conformed ever more closely to Christ until we attain true holiness" (*RVM*, 26).[12] We enter into the will of God.

Many of the great saints give us similar insight. See some of these themes in the excerpts below from St. Louis de Monfort's *True Devotion to Mary*, and note his reference to the words of another great saint, St. Augustine:

> St. Augustine, surpassing himself, and going beyond all I have yet said, affirms that all the predestinate, in order to be conformed to the image of the Son of God, are in this world hidden in the womb of the most holy Virgin, where they are guarded, nourished, brought up and made to grow by that good Mother until she has brought them forth to glory after death, which is properly the day of their birth, as the Church calls the death of the just.[13]

So beneficial is Mary's maternal solicitude toward her spiritual children that, de Montfort tells us, "when Mary has struck her roots in a soul, she produces there marvels of grace, which she alone can produce, because she alone is the fruitful Virgin who never has had, and never will have, her equal in purity and in fruitfulness."[14] He continues:

Mary has produced, together with the Holy Ghost, the greatest thing which has been or ever will be—a God-Man; and she will consequently produce the greatest saints that there will be in the end of time. The formation and the education of the great saints who shall come at the end of the world are reserved for her. For it is only that singular and miraculous Virgin who can produce, in union with the Holy Ghost, singular and extraordinary things.[15]

Entering the school of Mary is a matter not so much of learning *about* Jesus but rather, as St. John Paul II puts it, of "learning him" (*RVM*, 14). And of this Mary is our teacher, the *ezer* of the Holy Trinity, who serves the Divine Pleasure in bringing about the fullness of Christ's life in our souls. Through her maternal beatitude and tutelage, not only are we transformed, but we become a source of transformation for others, through whom the Divine Goodness is diffused to the world.[16]

AGENTS OF TRANSFORMATION: THE NEW EVANGELIZATION

Every encounter with Christ is transformative. All we need do is look at the interactions of Christ with people in Sacred Scripture, and we see this is the case. We need go no further than the call of the apostles, the raising of Lazarus from the dead, the transforming moment with the woman at the well, the great gift of mercy received by the woman caught in adultery, and the healings of the woman with the hemorrhage and the lame man at the pool of Siloam.[17] In each and every case, grace was offered, and grace was received. When we respond to the initiative of divine life Jesus offers us, new life is generated within us and then replicates itself in the lives of others.

In this we image God, the Three in One. "God is love," St. John tells us (1 John 4:16). And love is a dynamic. Love cannot be contained; it seeks outward expression. Love must be shared, and it does so through self-donative acts.

Think of an act of charity: helping a sick loved one, feeding the hungry, catechizing children, offering aid to storm victims or the victims of war and terror, visiting the imprisoned. All of these acts of love require the gift of self, from which new life and healing can spring forth in ourselves and in others. The source is the divine life that Christ's salvific action gives to us.

Gazing into the eyes of Jesus with Mary, opening ourselves to the presence of the mystery, entering into the mystery through the maternal tutelage of our mother who knows its secrets, we are changed, transformed. The inner confines of our heart are illuminated; the soul is enflamed with the love of God; the mind is purified and made new. Dr. Lilles writes, "When this fire from above enkindles the mind, something is communicated that is not merely informative, but transformative." He continues:

> Souls baptized in this hidden radiance often wonder whether they are wasting their time. And yet, mysteriously, their confidence and devotion are set ablaze with a love they cannot explain. This transformation is not limited to one's life but is extended throughout one's culture and continues to extend into the future.[18]

Thus contemplative prayer is generative. It vivifies the whole of the created world with a restorative and renewing reality that is passed from generation to generation. This is the living out of the grace of baptism and the holy work to which each of us is called by virtue of baptism. It is precisely what is most necessary "for such a time as this" (Esther 4:14).

The Call and Mission: A Sacred and Holy Trust

Throughout his letter on the Rosary, St. John Paul II repeatedly refers to the dire issues that plague contemporary man. He speaks to the challenges of contemporary culture—the threat to world peace, the threat of secularism, the threat of false ideologies, the many threats to family life—and the agonies, anxieties, and endeavors these thrust upon us. The solution he offers is the transforming power of the Rosary and the willingness to meet these challenges with the power of Christ.

Our call and mission, the holy trust that God enjoins upon us in our time, is to be a "sign of contradiction" in our world. We are to be like the Blessed Virgin Mary, who always points man and woman to Jesus Christ. As stated in the book *Experience Grace in Abundance*:

Through the power of the Holy Spirit operative in us, we are to imbue all of society and culture with the gospel message. We are to infuse a Christian spirit into the customs and mores of the social milieu. We are to establish gospel principles as the standard against which laws and ethics are weighed. We are to advance all of society's values that honor God and to eliminate those that do not. We are to bring a Christian perspective to public affairs, to mass media, to professional duties, and to domestic life. We are to infuse our schools, our parishes, our communities, and our social activities with the life of Jesus Christ.[19]

Transformed by Christ through the mysteries of His divine life, we are to transform the world. This unprecedented time in which we live calls for the type of saints that St. Louis de Montfort describes in *True Devotion*:

> The Most High with His Holy Mother has to form for Himself great saints who shall surpass most of the other saints in sanctity as much as the cedars of Lebanon outgrow the little shrubs...
>
> These great souls, full of grace and zeal, shall be chosen to match themselves against the enemies of God, who shall rage on all sides; and they shall be singularly devout to our Blessed Lady, illuminated by her light, strengthened with her nourishment, led by her spirit, supported by her arm and sheltered under her protection, so that they shall fight with one hand and build with the other. With one hand they shall fight, overthrow and crush heretics with their heresies, the schismatics with their schism, the idolaters with their idolatries and the sinners with their impieties. With the other hand they shall build [Nehemiah 4:17] the temple of the true Solomon and the mystical city of God, that is to say, the most holy Virgin, called by the Fathers the "Temple of Solomon" and the "City of God." By their words and their examples they shall draw

the whole world to true devotion to Mary. This shall bring
upon them many enemies, but shall also bring many victories and much glory for God alone....

...Teaching the narrow way of God in pure truth,
according to the holy Gospel, and not according to the
maxims of the world; troubling themselves about nothing;
not accepting persons; sparing, fearing, and listening to no
mortal, however influential he may be. They shall have in
their mouths the two-edged sword of the Word of God.
They shall carry on their shoulders the bloody standard of
the Cross, the Crucifix in their right hand and the Rosary
in their left, the Sacred Names of Jesus and Mary in their
hearts, and the modesty and mortification of Jesus Christ
in their own behavior. These are the great men who are
to come; but Mary is the one who, by order of the Most
High, shall fashion them for the purpose of extending His
empire over that of the impious, the idolaters, and the
Mahometans. But when and how shall this be? God alone
knows.[20]

In the following three chapters, you will meet some great
men and women who were willing to be "signs of contradiction" in their own day and time. By living out the grace of
their baptism, they preserved the seed of faith in their families, their communities, their culture, and even the Church.
Some lived to tell their story; others died on the battlefield in
their pursuit; all held up a standard for us to follow. May you
be inspired by them to do the same in this our day and time
that, as St. Louis de Montfort describes, we may bring many
victories and much glory for God alone.

A Rosary Story
Hail, Holy Queen
Dr. Scott Hahn

My earliest encounter with Marian devotion came when my Grandma Hahn passed away. She'd been the only Catholic on either side of my family—a quiet, humble, and holy soul. Since I was the only religious one in the family, my father gave me her religious articles when she died. I looked at them with horror. I held her Rosary in my hands and ripped it apart, saying, "God, set her free from the chains of Catholicism that have bound her." I meant it too. I saw the Rosary and the Virgin Mary as obstacles between Grandma and Jesus Christ.

Even as I slowly approached the Catholic faith—drawn inexorably by the truth of one doctrine after another—I could not accept the Church's Marian teaching. Yet despite all the scruples of my Protestant training, I took up the Rosary one day and began to pray. I prayed for a very personal, seemingly impossible intention. On the next day, I took up the beads again, and the next day and the next. Months passed before I realized that my intention, the seemingly impossible situation, had been reversed since the day I first prayed the Rosary. My petition had been granted.

From that moment, I knew my mother. From that moment, I believe, I truly knew my home in the covenant family of God. Yes, Christ was my brother. Yes, he'd taught me to pray "Our Father." Now, in my heart, I accepted His command to behold my mother (see John 19:27). I made the decision to let myself be her son.

Without a doubt, the Church's most popular and beloved expression of Marian devotion is the Rosary. It's my favorite expression too. Love engendering love—that's the secret of the Rosary.

I set aside time to pray the Rosary. But I also pray the Rosary when I find time that would otherwise be spent unproductively—when I'm stuck in a doctor's waiting room or delayed in rush-hour traffic. The rush hour is unreal in comparison to the reality of the Rosary, the mysteries of ultimate reality. My beads and my prayers are more real than the cars in front of me and the honking horns.

At one time, I looked at Grandma Hahn's Rosary beads and saw a noose that choked off true devotion in an otherwise godly woman. Now I look at my own beads and see a queen's crown, a mother's encircling arms.

Dr. Scott Hahn, an internationally renowned Catholic lecturer and apologist, is a professor of theology at Franciscan University of Steubenville in Steubenville, Ohio. This story is excerpted and adapted from his book Hail, Holy Queen: The Mother of God in the Word of God.

Chapter Seven

Your Special Forces Team

KNIGHTS OF THE KINGDOM

Few souls understand what God would accomplish
in them if they were to abandon themselves unre-
servedly to Him and if they were to allow His grace
to mold them accordingly. [1]

—ST. IGNATIUS OF LOYOLA

The mission God has entrusted to us would certainly
be formidable without the grace to accomplish it. But,
as the above quote by St. Ignatius reminds us, when we permit
ourselves to be molded by the grace of God, great things can
be accomplished in us and through us. The witness of the
saints proves as much and serves to encourage us to be more
than conquerors through Christ Jesus (Romans 8:31–39). We

would do well, then, to come to know these holy men and women, to seek their guidance and their prayerful intercession. In the next three chapters we will have the opportunity to meet at least some of them. Like all of us, they are part of the communion of saints. Though we profess belief in the communion of saints whenever we proclaim the Apostles' Creed, the concept is an enigma for many of us and a reality rarely explored. This is regrettable, because such a lack of consideration deprives us of one of the greatest treasures we have in the economy of God. The communion of saints is a wonderful resource for us as we face the tempests of life.

What then is the communion of saints? The *Catechism of the Catholic Church* describes *three states* within the communion of saints: those who are pilgrims on earth, those who have died and are being purified, and those who "are in glory contemplating 'in full light, God himself triune and one, exactly as he is'" (*CCC*, 954). These three states are commonly called the Church Militant, the Church Suffering, and the Church Triumphant, respectively.

Like all of the great mysteries and gifts of God, the communion of saints has a vast and encompassing meaning. The union of these three states in the Church is filled with a sense of family unity and love; intercession, camaraderie, and mutual aid; and a mystical bond between persons, distinguished only by state of salvation. While the mystery of this union is beyond full comprehension, to the extent we permit ourselves to enter into it through the gift of faith, we can begin to experience its benefits. We can "meet," if only spiritually, brothers and sisters in Christ who want to assist us on the battlefield of life.

The Saints: Our Battle Partners

In their book *The Warrior Soul*, authors Jerry Boykin and Stu Weber, both special forces members, recount a time they asked a retiring Delta Force commander what weapon he most wanted with him in battle. Without hesitation, the major general replied, "When I go into battle, I want a fellow warrior beside me who's big enough to carry me when I get hit!"[2]

Though this response speaks to the flesh-and-blood reality of a trained military expert, it also addresses a principle for those who engage in spiritual warfare: We need partners at our side, to wage war with us in the spiritual battles and skirmishes of our everyday life.

This is God's plan. He never abandons us, and he never sends us into battle alone. He always makes provision for us. God entrusted Eve to Adam as his *ezer kenegdo*, his battle partner, to aid and assist him in the Garden of Eden; when Jesus sent the apostles out into the world, he sent them out in pairs; and from the cross, Our Lord bequeathed to us His own mother to be our advocate and to distribute to us the graces we need to win the victory. And, as we know, God assigns to each of us a guardian angel as our battle partner.

God knows the enemy, and he sees the battle we are in as the Church Militant, facing "the flaming darts of the evil one" (Ephesians 6:16). He wants us to win, so he provides all that is necessary for that triumph. His provision includes the great cloud of witnesses known as the communion of saints. Our brothers and sisters of the Church Triumphant stand next to us as our battle partners in this war zone called life.

Let's meet some of these amazing saints. In this chapter, we will look at some of the great knights of the kingdom who fought valiantly on behalf of God. In the next, we will meet some valiant women of the Church who did likewise.

St. Joseph, Terror of Demons (First Century)
Patron of families and workers
FEAST DAYS: ST. JOSEPH, HUSBAND OF MARY, MARCH 19;
AND ST. JOSEPH THE WORKER, MAY 1

"The prayer of the righteous is powerful and effective."
—James 5:16, NRSV

One of our most formidable battle partners is St. Joseph, husband of the Mother of God and foster father of the Messiah. An icon of righteousness, he exemplified the virtues to a superlative degree. As the Litany of St. Joseph attests, he was "Joseph most just,… most chaste,… most prudent,… most strong,… most obedient,… most faithful." These virtues were the armor and weaponry he used to protect the Holy Family. And he used them well: The litany calls him "Terror of demons"![3]

Note Joseph's courage, trust, and obedience after learning of Mary's pregnancy (Matthew 1:18–24). According to Fr. Marie-Dominique Phillipe, OP, Joseph never questioned

Mary's loyalty to him or her faithfulness to God. Rather, he realized that in Mary God was fulfilling the prophesy of Isaiah 7:1, "Behold, the virgin shall conceive and bear a son." Though they were betrothed, Joseph decided to "send her away quietly" so God's will could be done in her and through her. But an angel of the Lord appeared to him in a dream and told him to have no fear in taking Mary as his wife. Some theologians say this is Joseph's annunciation and the "test" of his fidelity to God.[4]

Of this test, Father Phillipe, OP, writes in his book, *The Mystery of Joseph*:

> [Joseph] accepts that God has brought about His masterpiece within Mary, without including him, her spouse. He accepts that Mary alone will be the source of life for the formation of the body of the Son of the Most High become man, and he is even glad, because Mary is thus fully glorified and takes precedence over him: she is first.... This is where we touch upon the most profound aspect of Joseph's holiness: his love for Mary is so great that it now compels him to look at nothing else but the Father's will for her.[5]

Paul Thigpen, writing in his book, *Saints Who Battled Satan*, states it succinctly:

> Joseph stood firm in his confidence that God had spoken and that God speaks only the truth.... He received the heavenly instructions in faith, just as Mary had done.[6]

Joseph's spiritual mettle is tested yet again through another message the angel brings him as he sleeps. The angel tells him,

"Get up, take the child, and his mother, and flee" (Matthew 2:13, *NRSV*). Herod, the Roman client king of Judea, is in a rage upon learning that a new king has been born in Bethlehem. In desperate fear for his position, he has ordered the execution of all the young male children in that vicinity.

St. Joseph promptly heeds the angel's instruction, gathering his family and setting out on the long and arduous journey to Egypt. His prudence and docility assure the safety of the Christ Child and His mother. The plans of the enemy are foiled.

Scripture gives us only a few other glimpses of the spiritual warfare Joseph endured while fulfilling his vocation as the foster father of Jesus: his struggle to find shelter for Mary on the night of Jesus's birth, the concern he must have experienced for his wife and child when he heard Simeon's dire prophecy, and the fear he must have felt when the adolescent Jesus was lost in the temple. Mary no doubt relied upon Joseph's fortitude in those moments and in countless others.

Throughout his life, Joseph bore virtue as his impenetrable armor. It protected him from harm, held him fast against the wiles and tactics of the devil, and won for him the ultimate victory.

SAINTLY TAKEAWAY: We would do well to ask St. Joseph for his intercession as we face the vicissitudes of life in today's world. And we would do well to grow in the virtues he emulated, so we can stand strong in the face of temptation and trial. What one virtue exemplified by Joseph is most urgent for you in this moment?

St. Michael the Archangel, Invincible Warrior[7]

Patron of soldiers, doctors, and police officers

FEAST OF THE HOLY ARCHANGELS, ALSO KNOWN AS
MICHAELMAS: SEPTEMBER 29

"And war broke out in heaven; Michael and his angels
fought against the dragon."
—Revelation 12:7, NRSV

The heavens are said to be filled with a myriad of angels who possess preternatural powers beyond the comprehension of the mortal mind. We know but a few by name, and one is the magnificent Michael, "Prince of the heavenly hosts," whose name means "Who is like unto God?"

Four times Michael is specifically mentioned in Scripture. Daniel mentions him as "one of the chief princes" who came to the defense of the kingdom of Persia (Daniel 10:13) and also as "the great prince" and "protector of [the] people who will arise" at the end of the world and the time of the Antichrist (Daniel 12:1). The Epistle of St. Jude tells us that "Michael contended with the devil and disputed about the body of Moses," telling Satan, "The Lord rebuke you!" (Jude 1:9). Finally, in the book of Revelation, we read "war arose in heaven, Michael and his angels fighting against the dragon" (Revelation 12:7).

Michael is the consummate combatant, assigned by the Church with four main tasks:

The first is to fight Satan. This he has done with exceptional skill. He proved his prowess in that first and great battle that resulted in Lucifer being tossed out of heaven and has battled with us ever since. Michael will take on Satan in yet another epic battle: At the end of time, he will defeat the Antichrist.

The second is to defend Christians from the Evil One. We know of many instances in which Michael played a pivotal role in the protection of God's people. When a plague nearly depopulated the city of Rome in AD 600, Michael appeared to Pope St. Gregory I during a procession. Michael thrust his sword into his scabbard to symbolize defeat of the plague, which stopped shortly thereafter. Centuries later, St. Joan of Arc would say that it was St. Michael who guided her in battle against the English during the Hundred Years' War.

Third, Michael champions the Church as her special protector. He is believed to have been the protector of God's people in the Old Testament and of Christians in the New Testament. Throughout Church history, Michael has been sent to give victory to the Church and remind her "the powers of death shall not prevail against it" (Matthew 16:18).

One stunning example of this occurred in 1884, when St. Michael appeared to Pope Leo XIII in a terrifying vision. In that vision, evil spirits were attacking the Church with cruel ferocity, but in the end, St. Michael cast Satan and his legions into the abyss. After recovering from the vision, the pope composed the now famous St. Michael Prayer, which calls upon him to "defend us in battle" and to "be our protection against the wickedness and snares of the devil."

Finally, Michael calls men's souls away from earth and brings them to judgment, which is why he is sometimes depicted holding the Book of Life or a pair of scales. It is also the duty of St. Michael to rescue the souls of the faithful from the power of the enemy, especially at the hour of death.[8]

Now more than ever, the Church and her faithful are in need of a warrior like Michael, whose spiritual valor sets an example to be emulated. By the grace of God, may he defend us all, that the gates of hell may not prevail against us.

St. Michael, invincible warrior, pray for us.

SAINTLY TAKEAWAY: Make a commitment to pray the St. Michael Prayer at least once a day and to use it when you are under attack or struggling:

St. Michael the archangel, defend us in battle.

Be our protection against the wickedness and snares of the devil.

May God rebuke him, we humbly pray.

And do thou, O Prince of the heavenly host, by the power of God, cast into hell Satan and all the evil spirits who prowl about the world seeking the ruin of souls. Amen.

St. George, the Great Martyr (c. 275–303)
Patron of soldiers, cavalry, and chivalry
FEAST DAY: APRIL 23.

And on his breast a bloody cross he bore,
The dear remembrance of his dying Lord,
For whose sweet sake that glorious badge he wore,
And dead (as living) ever him adored. [9]
—Edmund Spenser, *The Faery Queen*

In every era, God raises up holy men and women to battle the evils of their day and time. Often putting their lives on the line, they speak truth when it is likely to be rejected; they act with courage when many would run away; they press forward when the majority would pack it in. Of all of these illustrious combatants, St. George is one of the most legendary.

Known as the "great martyr" and "the dragon slayer," it is believed he was born in Cappadocia in approximately AD 275. He became a soldier in the army and, though Christian, is said to have been a favorite of the fiercely anti-Christian Roman Emperor Diocletian.

In AD 302, Diocletian issued an edict ordering the arrest of every Christian solider in his army. With his characteristic courage and zeal, George faced the emperor in the presence of his fellow soldiers and proclaimed himself a Christian. So fond of St. George was the emperor that he attempted to bribe the saint with gifts of land, money, and slaves, but St. George vehemently refused to deny Christ.

Thus began one of the most protracted campaigns of torture in the history of the Church. George was stretched on the rack, his flesh ripped with hooks, and salt poured into his open wounds. When that didn't convince him to renounce Christ, he was pressed into a box that was pierced with nails, impaled on sharp stakes, and plunged into boiling water. Then the torturers attacked his head with a hammer. George remained firm in his faith.

According to legend, God comforted George in prison and told him he would die three "deaths" before entering Paradise. The first of these deaths involved a magician named Athanasius, whom the emperor ordered to concoct a potion to kill George. George drank the potion, and nothing happened. Athanasius gave him another cup of the poison, and again

George was unscathed. Impressed, Athanasius confessed Christ on the spot and was executed.

The next day, George faced his second "death." He was tossed into a well that was sealed with a stone. Heaven intervened. God appeared with the archangel Michael, who freed the saint. The officer in charge was immediately converted, along with eleven hundred other soldiers and one woman. They too were summarily executed.

Diocletian attempted to kill George a third time with even more gruesome tortures. But to the fury of the emperor, at day's end the saint was still alive.

The emperor tried again to persuade George to sacrifice to Apollo. The saint appeared to relent, which won him an invitation to the palace that evening. There, George engaged in conversation with Alexandra, the emperor's wife. She was converted and subsequently martyred.

Finally, after suffering scores of the cruelest punishments known to man, George knew his end was near. He quickly arranged for his earthly possessions to be distributed to the poor. He was beheaded on April 23 in the year 303.

The image of St. George slaying a dragon is symbolic of the life and death of this great warrior of God. Some claim the dragon symbolizes Satan, and the young "damsel in distress" shown in some images symbolizes God's truth.

St. George is one of the Fourteen Holy Helpers, a group of saints venerated for the efficacy of their intercession. He is a great saint for our day and time, when we too need to slay dragons in our midst for the sake of God's truth.

St. George, Great Martyr, pray for us.

SAINTLY TAKEAWAY: St. John Paul II reminds us that God may offer us the crown of martyrdom. Make it a daily practice to pray for the grace of final perseverance should you be offered so great an honor.

St. Ignatius of Loyola, Father General (1491–1556)
Founder of the Jesuits, the Society of Jesus
FEAST DAY: JULY 31

Ad majorem Dei gloriam ("All for the greater glory of God")

As a young man, St. Ignatius of Loyola longed to be a great soldier and achieve fame on the battlefields of Europe. He was destined to engage in a much loftier war than one fought on turf and terra. His battlefield would be that of the spirit.

Born Iñigo Lopez de Loyola in 1491, he was the youngest of thirteen children. His mother died soon after he was born. As a young aristocrat, Ignatius aspired to military exploits, ambitions fed by his avid reading of the knights of Camelot and the adventures of El Cid. As soon as the opportunity arose, he joined the army. By the age of seventeen, he was known to strut about "with his cape slinging open to reveal his tight-fitting hose and boots; a sword and dagger at his waist."[10]

But Iñigo's swashbuckling escapades came to an abrupt end in 1521, when during the Battle of Pamplona, he was seriously injured by a cannon ball. During his convalescence, he read *The Life of Christ* by Rudolph of Saxony, and his soul caught fire for Jesus, King of Kings. He was filled with a holy zeal to lead a life of self-denial and emulate the heroic deeds of the great monastics.

When Iñigo recovered from his injuries, he undertook a pilgrimage to Our Lady of Montserrat, a shrine in the mountains above Barcelona. Upon arriving, he left his sword on the altar and donned sackcloth. He made a full confession and promised to lead a life of penance and devotion to God. Later, he retired to a nearby cave, where for nearly a year he lived a life of prayer, penance, and poverty.

During this time, Ignatius suffered a severe trial of scruples, which lead to depression and a sadness that at times tempted him toward suicide. He began noting his inner thoughts and experiences, which eventually became his famous *Spiritual Exercises*. Underlying these exercises is discernment of spirits to discover God's will. Of key importance is the awareness of the interior movements of the heart, as well as the guiles of Satan. St. Ignatius taught that the enemy scatters innumerable demons throughout the world to ensnare men and women.

When peace finally returned to him, Ignatius embarked on a brief pilgrimage to the Holy Land, then returned to Europe, where he attended university. There he met six key companions whom he instructed in the *Exercises*.

On the morning of August 15, 1534, in the Church of St. Peter, at Montmartre, France, Loyola and his six companions voiced solemn vows. In 1539, they became the Society of Jesus, more commonly known as the Jesuits.

St. Ignatius is a particularly powerful battle partner because of his experience in discerning the ways of God and the ways of the enemy. In the perpetual war for the souls of man, he is a master strategist. During his lifetime, demons who possessed people would sometimes cry out at the mere mention of his name, "Ignatius is my greatest enemy!"[11]

The Spiritual Exercises of St. Ignatius have taught the faithful for centuries how to "polish" and "sharpen" their weapons. His teachings lead Christians to a robust interior life and a sincere pursuit of Christian perfection.

St. Ignatius of Loyola, Father General, pray for us.

SAINTLY TAKEAWAY: In the discerning process, St. Ignatius tells us to heed the movements of the heart to know God's will. Does your consideration of a decision bring you consolation (think of the fruit of the Holy Spirit in Galatians 5:22) or desolation (the opposite of the fruits of the Holy Spirit)? Go with the choice that brings you consolation, but do nothing until you have clarity.

St. Louis IX, Lieutenant of God(1214–1270)
Patron of Secular Franciscans and France
FEAST DAY: AUGUST 25
"A son cannot refuse to obey his father."

The only canonized king of France, St. Louis was just twelve years old when he was crowned and only twenty-one when he assumed full authority of the kingdom from his mother. While others of his age and status were enjoying the frivolity of court life, Louis was already groomed as a great warrior in the eyes of God and man.

Thanks to his mother, Blanche, Louis had great love and esteem for all that is holy. She once told him: "I love you, my dear son, as much as a mother can love her child; but I would rather see you dead at my feet than that you should ever commit a mortal sin."[12]

This great love for God became the motivating factor of Louis's life, guiding him in all the complexities of managing the largest army and wealthiest kingdom in all of Europe. Everything he did was for the glory of God—from strategizing with military leaders to securing the borders, from negotiating with foreign rulers to dispensing justice. Renowned for his charity, he took care of the poor and the marginalized. He was particularly known for his leniency, even to those who rebelled against him.

Louis's interior strength came from his great devotion to the Holy Sacrifice of the Mass, which he attended twice a day. His heart was firmly committed to serving God. He established himself as the quintessential Christian monarch, saintly and fair in all his dealings, both on the world stage and in his own home.

Louis married Margaret, a pious woman, and the couple was blessed with eleven children. The queen shared Louis's devotion to God, and the couple were also devoted to each other. They enjoyed riding together, reading, listening to music, and all that was involved in the daily practice of the faith.

Perhaps the greatest insight we have into the heart of this holy king comes from a letter of advice that he penned to his eldest son, Philip III. Louis urged Philip to avoid all mortal sin and to love God with all his heart and strength. He instructed him to be kindhearted toward the poor and to be just toward his subjects, "swaying, neither to right nor left, but holding the line of justice." Most importantly, he wrote: "Be devout and obedient to our mother the Church of Rome and the Supreme Pontiff as your spiritual father. Work to remove all sin from your land, particularly blasphemies and heresies."[13]

A warrior at heart, when Louis was still in his mid-thirties, he embarked on a six-year crusade to Egypt, which had become the base of Muslim power in the world. On April 6, 1250, he lost his army at the Battle of Al Mansurah and was captured by the Egyptians, who demanded an enormous ransom for his release.

Louis spent four more years traveling through the Latin kingdoms, using his great wealth to assist the Crusaders and conducting diplomacy with the Islamic powers of Syria and Egypt. He returned to his throne in the spring of 1254.

Louis's desire to promote the kingdom of God on earth led him on yet another Crusade in 1267, when he and his three sons "took up the cross" and headed for Tunis. The campaign ended tragically when disease broke out in the camp. Dysentery carried off many fighters, including the king, who died on August 25, 1270. He was canonized a brief twenty-seven years later.

St. Louis IX, Lieutenant of God, pray for us.

SAINTLY TAKEAWAY: St. Louis IX knew that true success flows from union with the will of God. Therefore, God's will was always his chief concern. Is there something you need to bring into conformity with the will of God?

St. Francis de Sales, Defender of Truth (1567–1622)

Patron of writers and publishing

FEAST DAY: JANUARY 24

"The measure of love is to love without measure."[14]

Known as the "Gentleman Saint," St. Francis de Sales had the steel will of a true warrior. The first of thirteen children born to an aristocratic father and his well-bred wife, Francis was frail at birth. His devoted mother, only fifteen years old at the time of his birth, gave him exceptional care and educated him until he could be tutored.

A bright student, at fourteen Francis was sent to the University of Paris, where his heart became set on serving God. He had consecrated himself to the Church at the age of eight, and now he was ready to live what he had promised. He took a vow of perpetual chastity and placed himself under the protection of the Blessed Virgin Mary.

Soon Francis experienced an unrelenting dark night of the soul. Fearing he had lost God's favor, he made a heroic act of love for God:

> O Lord, if I am never to see Thee in Heaven, this at least grant me, that I may never curse or blaspheme Thy holy name. If I may not love Thee in the other world—for in Hell none praise Thee—let me at least every instant of my brief existence here love Thee as much as I can.[15]

His fear instantly disappeared, and Francis was filled with peace. This experience would later guide him in directing similarly afflicted souls.

Francis attended law school at the University of Padua and returned home upon graduation. It was quickly apparent that the life of nobility held no allure for him. Disappointed, his father only relented to his vocation when Francis was offered the position of provost for the chapter of cathedral canons. Within six months, he was ordained a priest.

The warrior in Francis's heart awakened when he volunteered for a missionary assignment in Savoy. It would lead to genuine spiritual combat. Protestant militants had invaded the area sixty years earlier, and only a handful of Catholics remained. The bishop of Geneva had been asked to send missionaries there to reclaim souls for the Church.

It was a dangerous assignment for priests. Anti-Catholic sentiment ran high. Armed garrisons were needed for protection at night. The first priest had withdrawn out of fear. Accompanied by his cousin, Canon Louis de Sales, Francis set out in September of 1594. The first thing the missionaries did on their arrival was to visit the twenty-some Catholics who still lived there. Then they expanded their territory to the flock in more remote villages.

Francis began to publicly debate Calvinist preachers and to write and distribute leaflets comparing Calvinism to Church teaching. His talks became popular as did the briefs, which were later collected into a book entitled *Controversies*.

Francis also offered spiritual direction and Catholic instruction to anyone who requested it. Before long, many lapsed Catholics were returning to the faith. His door and his heart were open to anyone who wished to explore the Church. His sermons, brilliant mind, and unfailing humility won the area back to the Catholic Church.

In 1602, Francis became the bishop of Geneva. In addition to the rigors of his new duties, he instituted catechetical studies in his diocese, often teaching the classes himself, and he continued to advise and direct souls. One of his directees was St. Jane Frances de Chantal, with whom he would found the Order of the Visitation. Another was his cousin by marriage, Madame de Chamoisy. His famous book *Introduction to the Devout Life* was compiled from letters of direction he wrote to her. It remains in print to this day.

Francis was only fifty-six years old when he died of a cerebral hemorrhage on December 28, 1622, the Feast of the Holy Innocents. The last word he spoke was one of advice to a religious sister. "Humility," he told her. His greatest weapon, and the sword with which he fought for the life of every soul who came to him for help, was his tremendous love for God. He was canonized in 1665 and proclaimed a doctor of the Church in 1877.

St. Francis de Sales, guide to truth, pray for us.

SAINTLY TAKEAWAY: Two characteristics that made St. Francis a great warrior for the kingdom were perseverance and humility. How are you nurturing these virtues in your life of faith?

St. Isidore of Seville Apostle of Grace
Patron of the Internet (560–636)
FEAST DAY: APRIL 4
"Teaching unsupported by grace may enter the ears,
but it never reaches the heart."[16]

Known as "the last scholar of the ancient world,"[17] the brilliant St. Isidore of Seville was born into an influential family of saints. One might deduce from such origins that his childhood was peaceful and happy, but that wasn't the case—at least not in the beginning.

Isidore was born to Severianus and Theodora in Cartagena, Spain, in AD 560. His parents were members of a family that played a vital role in converting the Visigothic kings from Arianism to Catholicism. They were blessed with a strong faith. Isidore's older brother, St. Leander of Seville, would serve as an archbishop. His younger brother, St. Fulgentius of Cartagena, would also grow up to be a bishop, and his sister, St. Florentina, became a religious.

Unfortunately, life didn't seem nearly as promising for the young Isidore. He found himself under the tutelage of his brother Leander, who used force when it came to his education. To this day, historians wonder why St. Leander was so hard on his younger brother, who was a naturally intelligent and hardworking boy.

The day finally came when Isidore had enough of this abuse and ran away from home. He was dogged by feelings of rejection and failure. Why couldn't he learn as quickly as Leander wanted?

In a moment of divine intervention, Isidore noticed a nearby rock that had been worn away by the slow drip of water. He noticed that even though the drops appeared to have little effect on the hard surface, the steady drip of the water had worn holes in the rock. It suddenly dawned on him that if he persevered in his studies, his brother's heart might eventually soften toward him, wearing away the hardness like so much dripping water on the cold, hard rock.

Isidore returned home and patiently endured his punishment, which was to be locked in a cell in order to prevent him from running away again. And from that moment on, he embraced his studies and mastered them. Despite the harshness of his earlier experiences, Isidore looked up to his brother, who helped him develop a strong commitment to prayer, study, and service of the Church.

The two also collaborated in converting the heretical Visigoths who had invaded Spain. When St. Leander died around AD 600, Isidore succeeded him as archbishop of Seville. There he labored to help the barbarian tribes assimilate into the culture and institutions of the Western Roman Empire.

One of Isidore's greatest efforts was to use education to counteract the increasing influence of Gothic barbarism throughout his episcopate. Isidore established seminaries in every diocese in the country. All branches of knowledge, including the arts and medicine, were taught, and the Christian faith was preserved.

Isidore's early experiences with Leander made a lasting impression on him. Perhaps because of his brother's autocratic rule with his education, Isidore understood the role grace plays in transforming the human intellect. "When God's grace does touch our innermost minds to bring understanding, then his word, which is received by the ear, can sink deep into the heart."[18]

Isidore's slow but steady efforts eventually paid off in the near eradication of Arianism, along with a strengthening of religious discipline throughout his see. He died at the age of seventy-eight, on April 4, 636. He was canonized and proclaimed a doctor of the Church by Pope Innocent XIII in 1722.

In 1997 Pope John Paul II declared St. Isidore the patron saint of the Internet due to his *Etymologiae*, a twenty-volume compendium covering a wide range of disciplines, including theology, medicine, law, beasts and birds, stones and metals, agriculture, houses, clothing, and furniture, to name a few. The work was said to contain "practically everything that it is necessary to know."[19]

St. Isidore of Seville, man of grace, pray for us!

SAINTLY TAKEAWAY: Early on, St. Isidore learned the importance of the virtue of constancy, something every warrior needs to acquire. To what extent is this a virtue you possess?

A Rosary Story
The Healing Mysteries
DION DIMUCCI

I came to the Rosary pretty late in life. My family was Catholic—because we were Italian, and everyone in our neighborhood was Catholic. So I took the faith for granted. It was part of the scenery, and the Rosary was part of the faith.

We DiMuccis weren't "the family that prays together," the kind Father Patrick Peyton promoted on the radio as he prayed the Rosary. Our dial was tuned to a different station. I was listening to Hank Williams and Howling Wolf. We got to church for weddings and funerals, but not much else.

Even so, weddings and funerals make a powerful impression. I remember when I was small, sitting in church and hearing people pray the Our Father and Hail Marys. Even then, I knew something mysterious and powerful was happening. I'd see the Rosary beads in the hands of the guy in the casket, and I knew they were important. When I got confirmed, my pastor gave me a set of my own.

Long story short: As a teen, I got into gang life and got addicted to drugs. I also started singing and became famous, with a long string of hits. The hits made me rich, but my life was a wreck. In the late 1960s, I encountered Jesus, and everything changed. I got clean and sober, and I started going to evangelical churches.

My life got pretty good. But I still needed healing. A guy who's an addict for fourteen years does damage to his body but also to his mind, his soul, his memories, and his relationships. I asked Jesus to give me a sure cure, and He heard my prayer. Eventually He led me back to the practice of the Catholic faith, and then to the Rosary.

At first the Rosary didn't turn me on. After years away from the Catholic Church, it seemed mindless and routine. Yet I could see the difference it made in the people who prayed it. Gradually those folks led me to understand it as a way of meditating on the mysteries of Jesus's life.

What got me hooked, though, was my discovery of the Healing Mysteries. They're not part of the usual set, but they helped me to see the things I really needed in my life. From the people who got healed in the Gospels, I learned to ask for good things. Here are the mysteries I would reflect upon each day as I took my morning walk:

- Jesus Heals the Centurion's Servant (Matthew 8)
- Jesus Heals a Man Possessed by Demons (Mark 1)
- Jesus Heals a Paralyzed Man (Mark 2)
- Jesus Heals a Man Blind Since Birth (John 9)
- Jesus Raises Lazarus from the Dead (John 11:17–45)

Day by day, I began to experience the healing I needed. I know that recovery is a lifelong process; Jesus isn't done with me yet, and He won't be until my days on earth are over. But till then, I'll be working the beads, and He'll be working His healing.

Praying the Rosary gives me peace, strength, and a stronger sense of family, with Jesus my brother and

Mary our mother. I pray that you will experience this same sense of healing and love as you reflect upon these mysteries too.

Dion DiMucci is a multiplatinum recording artist, Grammy nominee, and inductee in the Rock and Roll Hall of Fame. His hits include "Abraham, Martin, and John," "Runaround Sue," and "The Wanderer." He co-authored (with Mike Aquilina) Dion: The Wanderer Talks Truth.

Chapter Eight

Your Special Forces Team

VALIANT WOMEN OF THE KINGDOM

By defending the dignity of women and their vocation, the Church has shown honor and gratitude for
those women who—faithful to the Gospel—have
shared in every age in the apostolic mission of the
whole People of God. They are the holy martyrs,
virgins, and mothers of families, who bravely bore
witness to their faith and passed on the Church's
faith and tradition by bringing up their children in
the spirit of the Gospel.

—POPE ST. JOHN PAUL II,
MULIERIS DIGNITATEM, 27

We have just looked at some great knights of the
kingdom, who inspire us to preserve and protect all

that is holy and God-honoring. Their witness too inspires us to persevere in all of our personal battles "against the powers, against the world rulers of this present darkness" (Ephesians 6:12). These men of honor hold up for us a double standard: one to holiness of life, the other to faithful adherence to Christ, His Church, and Mary, the Mother of God.

The history of Holy Mother Church also shines with the witness of many women who soldiered forward in the midst of great trials, persecutions, and attacks from the Evil One and his minions. Exercising the authentic authority and power that derive from the charisms of their femininity, these daughters of the Most High God accomplished feats that stunned clerics as well as the common man. "Not by might, nor by power, but by My Spirit, says the Lord of hosts" (Zechariah 4:6) could well have been their battle cry.

Like their masculine counterparts, these valiant women could fill entire libraries with their stories of holiness and courage. Here are just a few accounts. We begin with the Blessed Virgin Mary under her title of Our Lady of Guadalupe. She is the woman of Genesis 3:15, the New Eve, who would smite the head of the serpent.

Our Lady of Guadalupe, Mother and Queen
Patroness of the Americas and of the unborn
FEAST DAY: DECEMBER 12
"Am I not your mother?"

The Aztec people of the early sixteenth century were remarkably advanced. Their empire was orderly and well managed, their towns filled with accomplished mathematicians, astronomers, architects, and physicians. Their judicial system was similar to that of Europe, and their children were educated from an early age.

The Aztecs, however, were a superstitious people. They made idols of the forces of nature, worshipping these as gods and goddesses in massive pyramidal temples at the centers of their towns. In their quest to attract beneficial forces and repel malevolent ones, they relied upon practices such as human sacrifice offered by black-robed priests, who tore out the beating hearts of living victims.[1] Millions were sacrificed to these elemental gods before the Spanish Captain Hernando Cortes arrived in 1519 and began to introduce the masses to the Christian faith.

This was the world into which Our Lady descended on the morning of December 9, 1531, when she appeared on Tepeyac Hill to a poor Mexican peasant and Christian convert named Juan Diego. Dressed as an Aztec princess and speaking in the Aztec language of Nahuatl, she identified herself as the "mother of the very true deity" and asked Juan to have a church built at the site.

> All those who sincerely ask my help in their work and in their sorrows will know my Mother's Heart in this place. Here I will see their tears; I will console them and they will be at peace. So run now to Tenochtitlan and tell the Bishop all that you have seen and heard.[2]

Juan Diego obeyed. He waited for hours to see Bishop-elect Fray Juan de Zumarraga, who was noncommittal on hearing the request. Disappointed, Juan Diego returned to find Our Lady waiting at the same spot, and he asked her to send someone else. "My little son," she said, "there are many I could send. But you are the one I have chosen."

Our Lady sent Juan back to the bishop, who once again kept him waiting, then asked him to provide a sign that the Lady he was seeing truly was the Blessed Virgin Mary. Reluctantly, Juan delivered the message to the lady, who smiled. "My little son, am I not your Mother? Do not fear," she consoled him. "The Bishop shall have his sign. Come back to this place tomorrow. Only peace, my little son."[3]

Juan Diego did not return the next day. His uncle had fallen mortally ill, and Juan Diego would remain by his side for two days, finally leaving to find a priest. This task required him to pass by Tepeyac Hill. Not wishing to have his journey slowed down even by the beautiful lady, Juan Diego tried to circumvent her by journeying via the mountain's opposite side. Much to his surprise, Mary was waiting there to speak to him.

> Do not be distressed, my littlest son. Am I not here with you who am your Mother? Are you not under my shadow and protection? Your uncle will not die at this time. There is no reason for you to engage a priest, for his health is restored at this moment. He is quite well. Go to the top of the hill and cut the flowers that are growing there. Bring them then to me.[4]

Despite the freezing weather, Juan Diego found the hillside abloom with Castilian roses. Removing his tilma, he filled it with flowers and brought them back to Our Lady, who carefully arranged them before sending him back to the bishop. "This time the Bishop will believe all you tell him," she assured him.

And so it was. Juan Diego found the bishop and several of his advisors at the palace. He was invited in, and he promptly opened his tilma to let the flowers fall to the floor. The bishop fell to his knees. Inside the peasant's robe was an exquisite image of the Blessed Virgin Mary, precisely as he had described her to the bishop.

At last the bishop agreed to build the church in honor of the Blessed Mother, Our Lady of Guadalupe. The miraculous image was displayed there for all to see. Through the centuries, the original church was expanded and replaced many times. The most recent Basilica of Our Lady of Guadalupe was consecrated on October 12, 1976.

Tens of millions of pilgrims have journeyed to Mexico City to venerate the miraculous image of Our Lady of Guadalupe, which remains as vibrant and awe-inspiring today as it was the moment heaven imprinted it on Juan Diego's tilma. The image has been the cause of millions of conversions as well. Within just six years of the apparition, almost nine million Aztecs were converted to Christianity.

In this, our day, when the idols of past and present are drawing souls away from the one true God, we do well to implore Mary's prayerful intercession under her title of Our Lady of Guadalupe. Through her maternal beatitude, she will smite the serpents of our time and point the way to her Son, Our Lord Jesus Christ.

Our Lady of Guadalupe, who smites the head of the serpent, pray for us.

SAINTLY TAKEAWAY: Our Lady of Guadalupe tells Juan Diego to be troubled about nothing, that she is with him and protecting him. She says this to you too. What is your most recent struggle or battle? Take it to the Blessed Mother, and ask for her intercession. As she says to Juan Diego, "Do you need anything more?"

Sts. Perpetua and Felicity, Standards of the Kingdom (Third century)

Patrons of expectant mothers and barren women

FEAST DAY: MARCH 7

"The Lord is my strength and my song."

—Psalm 119:14

While the annals of the Church are full of examples of valiant Catholic women, few stories can rival the tale of two young mothers who showed such fierce courage in the face of death that even the hardest Roman soldiers were brought to their knees. Spiritual warriors, Perpetua and Felicity stand as great icons of the faith and have been an encouragement to the faithful throughout generations. Their story, recorded as "The Martyrdom of Perpetua and Felicity," so inspired the early Church that it was often read at liturgies.

The women graced the early third century of Carthage, a Roman province of North Africa. The twenty-two-year-old young mother named Vibia Perpetua decided to become Christian and was baptized. Because her conversion took place during the persecution of Septimius, the lives of this noblewoman and her newborn son were instantly in danger.

While nothing is known about her husband, Perpetua's father was frantic. He knew the potential cost of her conversion, and he was concerned for the safety and well-being of his daughter and grandson. However, it must be said that Satan will use even well-intentioned motives to work his evil will. He can snake his way into our lives even through those we love. And so it was with Perpetua.

Consumed with worry, her father tried to make her renounce her decision. Perpetua tried to help him understand, but it was to no avail.

> "Father," I said, "do you see, let's say, that the vessel lying here is a little pitcher? Or is it something else?"
>
> He replied, "I can see that it's a pitcher."
>
> So I asked him, "Can it be called by any other name than what it truly is?"
>
> "No," he replied.
>
> "Then neither can I call myself anything other than what I am: a Christian."
>
> My father, provoked by what I said, threw himself on me...overcome by the arguments of the Devil.[5]

Time and again, the Evil One used Perpetua's father to try to dissuade her from her commitment to Christ. What emotional and mental turmoil this caused Perpetua! But she remained steadfast, and not long after her announcement, she was arrested along with four other catechumens. Among them was the slave woman named Felicity, who was eight months pregnant.

The two women were tossed into a dark, overcrowded prison. The heat was suffocating, and light was so dim that Perpetua claimed she "had never known such darkness." Both she and Felicity were treated roughly by the soldiers, but nothing caused Perpetua more pain than being separated from her newborn baby.

Thanks to the intervention of two compassionate deacons, the women were moved to a better part of the prison, where Perpetua's family and her infant son could visit her. Eventually, the baby was permitted to stay, which had a transforming effect upon Perpetua. "My prison suddenly became a palace for me," she recorded in her journal.

Many attempts were made to make Perpetua renounce Christ. Even the prosecutor in charge of her case tried to convince her to change her mind for the sake of her father and son. But she refused. And so her execution was ordered.

Meanwhile, Felicity was desperate to give birth so she could be executed with her friends. She was relieved when labor began two days before the scheduled execution. It was a terrible experience for her. But when the guards taunted her, Felicity calmly responded, "Now I'm the one who is suffering, but in the arena Another will be in me suffering for me because I will be suffering for Him." She gave birth to a little girl, who was eventually adopted by a Christian woman.

Throughout this time, the power and strength of Perpetua and Felicity were so impressive that the prison warden was converted. And according to eyewitnesses on the day of their death, they and the other catechumens approached their martyrdom with joy and calm.

Once inside the arena, the two women were stripped to face a rabid heifer. However, the crowd was outraged to see that Felicity had just given birth, and so the women were removed and clothed once again. Upon reentering the arena, they gave each other the kiss of peace and stood side by side as they were attacked. But the animal didn't kill them; that would take a gladiator's sword.

Perpetua was first pierced between the ribs, and then, taking hold of the sword herself, she guided it to her throat. Her last words were to her brothers in the faith: "Stand fast in the faith and love one another. Do not let our sufferings be a stumbling block for you."

The story of the heroic martyrdom of Perpetua and Felicity has roused the hearts of Christians for nearly two thousand years. These two young mothers proved themselves fierce warriors for Christ. Their witness shows us the power of the gift of fortitude when engaged. It is this gift that "enables one to conquer fear, even fear of death, and to face trials and persecutions. It inspires one even to renounce and sacrifice his life in defense of a just cause" (*CCC*, 1808).

Let us all look to Perpetua and Felicity as examples of how to rely upon this gift, so we too might die for Christ should circumstances require it.

Saints Perpetua and Felicity, valiant women of God, pray for us.

SAINTLY TAKEAWAY: How did Perpetua and Felicity use their suffering and travail for the sake of the kingdom? In what ways do they inspire you to do the same?

St. Quiteria, Warrior for the Kingdom
(Fifth century)
Invoked for protection against rabies
FEAST DAY: MAY 22.

"Do not be conformed to this world but be transformed by
the renewal of your mind, that you may prove what is the
will of God, which is good and acceptable and perfect."

—Romans 12:2

Upholding truth and justice is nothing new to Church
history. Many Catholic saints have been great crusaders for
these ideals, such as St. Thomas More and St. Joan of Arc. A
popular Portuguese saint is another such warrior who literally
lost her head for Jesus Christ, the Church He founded, and
the teachings His Church proclaims.

Though much of her story may well be legend, it seems
St. Quiteria's extraordinary life began at the moment of her
birth. She was the first of nine baby girls (nonuplets) born
to the wife of an important military official in the town of
Meenya, Portugal. The girls' mother was disgusted by what
she considered to be a "litter" of babies. She feared she would
be compared to an animal or a lowly peasant. In order to
avoid that fate, she ordered her maid to keep the number of
births from her husband, and to drown the infants in the river.

Thanks be to God, the maid disobeyed. She and a neigh-
boring peasant woman resolved to raise the girls. All nine
were raised as Christians, and they all would become valiant
women for the kingdom.

As the girls grew to adulthood, their faith grew in strength.
Their consequent refusal to worship Roman gods eventually

brought them before their own father for judgment. When he saw them, he recognized their likeness to his wife and thus discovered the secret she had kept from him for so many years. He immediately resolved to take the girls into his home and marry them to well-bred Roman military men.

It would seem as if the story of Quiteria and her sisters was coming to a happy end, but this was not the case. The girls flatly refused to marry pagan worshipers. Hoping to persuade them, their father had the girls imprisoned in a tower. These resourceful young ladies managed not only to escape but to free all the other prisoners as well. The lot of them fled to the mountains, where they waged a guerilla war against the Roman Empire.

Their campaign was not successful. Quiteria was caught and beheaded on the spot. Her sister Euphemia found herself unable to escape the soldiers who pursued her, and rather than succumb to them, she threw herself off a cliff. Legend has it that a rock opened up and swallowed her, and a hot spring instantly emerged from the spot. Marina and Liberata were also martyred, and they are canonized saints. History does not tell us what happened to the others.

Often Quiteria is pictured holding her head in her hands, with two rabid dogs at her side. According to one Portuguese legend, the body of St. Quiteria was thrown into the sea, from which it emerged sometime later with head in hands. Another legend has her keeping two rabid dogs at bay by talking sweetly and softly to them.

Quiteria and her sisters are the perfect battle partners for those who feel pressured to conform to the world and the dictates of secularism. These nine women were not afraid to be different, knowing that this difference is precisely what challenges and attracts souls to the message of God. With just a handful of people, they waged war on the entire Roman Empire, taking to heart the words of St. Paul to the Romans, "Do not be conformed to this world but be transformed by the renewal of your mind, that you may prove what is the will of God, which is good and acceptable and perfect" (Romans 12:2). Only God knows how many hearts were touched, perhaps even converted, by the courageous stand of these women.

St. Quiteria, valiant woman, pray for us.

SAINTLY TAKEAWAY: The witness of St. Quiteria and her sisters encourages us to stand for the truths of the faith in this our day and time. Are you willing to take a stand for truth when friends and family oppose the teachings of the Church and Sacred Scripture?

St. Thérèse of Lisieux (Thérèse of the Child Jesus), Soldier of the Little Way (1873–1897)
Patron of France (with Joan of Arc)
and foreign missions (with Francis Xavier)
FEAST DAY: OCTOBER 1
"Each time that my enemy would provoke me to combat,
I behave as a gallant soldier."[6]

St. Thérèse, the Little Flower of Lisieux, is known for many things, such as her little way of spiritual childhood. But one of her most important characteristics—and the one that makes her the perfect battle partner for the weak-kneed—is her indomitable warrior spirit. Who would think that this precious saint carried within her heart the desire to fight mighty wars for the sake of Christ? Although she cherished her vocation as a Carmelite, spouse of Christ, and spiritual mother, she never hid this other desire that filled her heart.

Thérèse's longing to do great things for God began when she was just a child. "In my childhood, I dreamed of combating in the battlefield," she writes. "When I began to learn the history of France, I was enchanted with the deeds of Joan of Arc; I felt in my heart a desire and courage to imitate them."[7]

So great was this desire that the year before the Maid of Orleans was canonized, Thérèse wrote a play about her entitled *The Mission of Joan of Arc*. Photos show Thérèse in armor, playing the part of St. Joan. The same fire that consumed the life of Joan raged in the soul of Lisieux's Little Flower.

This desire would remain throughout her life. She speaks of it several times in her autobiography, *The Story of a Soul*. We can almost feel her passion when she pens,

> I feel the vocation of the WARRIOR, THE PRIEST, THE APOSTLE, THE DOCTOR, THE MARTYR.... O Jesus. I feel within my soul the courage of the *Crusader*, the *Papal Guard*, and I would want to die on the field of battle in defense of the Church.[8]

This fervor was far from the mindless ranting of an over-zealous soul. Thérèse *believed* with all of her heart that God, her beloved, *le bon Dieu*, loved her unconditionally. And it was from this firm belief that she drew her legendary confidence in Him. If God called her to war, He would provide her with everything she needed to conduct that war according to His holy will.

It was also this absolute confidence in God in and for all things that undergirded the spirituality of her Little Way. Her childlike soul was a jeweled coffer that housed all the power of heaven, acquired simply by her complete and total trust in God. This is why she insisted that, in the everyday struggles of the spiritual life, the faithful must not grow weary in the pursuit of holiness. She saw sanctity as "the tip of the sword" that was needed to fight.[9]

Even on her deathbed, with her strength sapped by tuberculosis, her fighting spirit never waned. As she lay dying, she lamented that she would have preferred to die in the arena with the name of Jesus on her lips.[10] Her last words spoke a truth that came from the very core of her being: "My God, I love thee."

Canonized on May 17, 1925, this twenty-four year old contemplative was declared a doctor of the Church on October 19, 1997. "Her ardent spiritual journey shows such maturity, and the insights of faith expressed in her writings are so vast and profound that they deserve a place among the great spiritual masters," declared Pope John Paul II.[11] Her wisdom and inspiration encourage us today to live for Christ and His truth.

St. Thérèse of Lisieux, soldier for Christ, pray for us.

SAINTLY TAKEAWAY: When God is seeking to help us grow in trust, he gives us situations and circumstances in which to *practice* it. How is he encouraging you today?

St. Joan of Arc, "The Maid of Orleans" (1412–1431)

Patroness of France and of soldiers
FEAST DAY: MAY 30
"I am not afraid. I was born to do this."[12]

An illiterate girl born of fifteenth-century peasantry in northeast France is the quintessential warrior-saint. Mystical visions inspired Joan of Arc to fight on behalf of an earthly king with the might bestowed upon her by the King of Kings. Known as the Maid of Orleans, Joan is most noted for her critical role in bringing Charles VII to the throne at the end of the Hundred Years' War and for the inglorious end of her life, tied to a pillar and engulfed in flames in Rouen, France.

Joan was about thirteen years old when she first heard the voice in her father's garden that would direct the course of her life. It seemed to come from the right, accompanied by a bright light. Frightened at first, Joan would come to know the voice as that of the archangel Michael, protector of France. He admonished Joan to govern herself well and to go to church often.

Over the next few years, Joan also heard the voices of St. Margaret and St. Catherine. They urged her to go to the king and tell him that God was sending her to give help to the kingdom and to see him crowned as king.

It was a precarious time in France. When Joan was born, Charles VI was on the throne, but bouts of insanity incapacitated him. His brother Louis, the Duke of Orleans, and his cousin, John the Fearless, the Duke of Burgundy, quarreled over the regency of France and the guardianship of the royal children. This dispute escalated to the point that the Duke of Burgundy arranged for the assassination of the Duke of Orleans. Meanwhile, Henry V of England took advantage of the discord and invaded France in 1415, capturing many northern towns.

Charles's son, Charles VII, assumed the title of dauphin at the age of fourteen.[13] John the Fearless was murdered under his command, and the new Duke of Burgundy, Philip the Good, aligned himself with the English in conquering large sections of France. Henry V decided to lay claim to the throne.

By the time Joan of Arc came to influence events, in 1429, nearly all of northern France and some parts of the southwest were under British control. Joan was fearful, questioning how a poor maid like herself could make a difference in the high-stakes war that was raging. She sought the aid of an uncle in obtaining permission to travel to Chinon to meet with the dauphin. She was rudely rebuffed, but her sheer persistence convinced authorities to allow the visit.

With her hair cropped short, dressed as a man, and accompanied by an armed escort, Joan appeared in the dauphin's court. On presenting herself to the king, she was heard to say, "Most noble Dauphin, I am come and am sent to you from God to give help to the kingdom and to you."[14]

The dauphin spoke with her privately, during which time "she confided to him a secret which was known to him alone and to God, which gave him a great confidence in her."[15] Joan would never reveal that secret, even at her trial.

After having Joan examined by theologians and others, the dauphin determined that she should "not be prevented from going to Orleans with the men-at-arms," because "to do otherwise would be resisting the Holy Spirit and making oneself unworthy of the help of God."[16]

Fitted with armor of steel, Joan soon marched with the army to Orleans. No one knows how she moved from being part of the army to being someone from whom generals sought counsel. However, before many days had passed, "she had inspired soldiers and captains with a new spirit of offensive and a conviction of victory: she had become their leader."[17] This leadership was undisputed.

Joan had an uncanny knowledge of all of the crafts of war. She knew how to bear a lance, assemble an army, order military operations, and direct artillery. It was said, "She showed as much wisdom and foresight as a captain who had fought for twenty or thirty years."[18]

She also led the expedition like a religious crusade. Priests marched and chanted the *Veni Creator Spiritus*. She made the soldiers stop swearing and go to Mass and confession.

Perhaps this is why victory after victory came to the armies of the dauphin. Before long, he was crowned in Rheims. A truce with England followed but didn't last long, and Joan was once again on the march. It would be her last. On May 23, 1430, near Compeign, she was ambushed and captured.

Imprisoned by the Burgundians at Beaurevoir Castle, Joan made several escape attempts and then was moved to Rouen. Here she was accused of heresy, subjected to a politically motivated trial, and condemned to die by burning.

On May 30, 1431, Joan was tied to a pillar at the Vieux-Marche in Rouen. Two priests held a crucifix before her, to which she affixed her gaze as the flames rose and consumed her body. She is said to have bowed her head and uttered the name of Jesus as she expired. Afterward, her executioners raked back the coals to expose her charred body, so none could claim that she had escaped. Then they burned the body twice more, reducing it to ashes, which they scattered on the Seine.

Pope Callixtus III ordered a retrial of Joan in 1452, at which she was cleared of all heresy charges. It would be another 464 years before she was canonized, on May 16, 1920, by Pope Benedict XV. Though the flames of hatred consumed her body, the flame of divine love ignited her soul with the brilliant fire of holy zeal.

St. Joan of Arc, quintessential warrior of God, pray for us.

SAINTLY TAKEAWAY: Joan's strength was her unshakable conviction that she was sent by God, and this faith proved contagious. How contagious is your faith? Do you need a "conviction boost"? Ask St. Joan of Arc to intercede for you.

St. Clare of Assisi, Fearless Woman of God
(1194–1253)
Patroness of television
FEAST DAY: AUGUST 11

Since the Lord has called us to such great things that
those who are to be a mirror and example to others
may be reflected in us, we are greatly bound to bless
and praise God and be all the more strengthened to
do good in the Lord.[19]

—St. Clare of Assisi

The mother of St. Clare of Assisi prayed fervently for a safe
delivery of her child. As she was doing so, the young countess
heard a voice say, "Do not be afraid, for you will joyfully bring
forth a clear light which will illuminate the world."[20] And so it
happened that on July 16, 1193, when Ortolana, wife of the
Count of Sasso-Rosso, gave birth to a little girl, she named
her *Chiara*, or Clare, which means "clear light."

Even as a young girl, Clare was dedicated to prayer. She was
eighteen when she heard St. Francis of Assisi preach during a
Lenten service. She was so moved that she sought his help in
following the Gospel more closely. Accompanied by her aunt
Bianca and another companion, she went to the chapel of the
Portiuncula to meet with Francis. At his orders, she joined the
convent of the Benedictine nuns of San Paulo. Before leaving
for the convent, she cut off her hair and donned a plain robe
and veil in place of her luxurious gown.

When Clare's father discovered what she had done, he
tracked her down and tried to force her back into his home.
Clare refused, saying she would have no husband other than
Jesus Christ. She clung to the convent altar until her father
gave up and went home without her. The time had come for
the prophecy about Clare to be fulfilled.

Francis eventually sent her to another Benedictine monastery, where she was soon joined by her younger sister, Catarina. Again the count determined to fetch his daughter, this time sending a squadron of armed kinsmen to bring Catarina home.[21] When she refused, her uncle drew his sword so as to strike her, but his arm suddenly dropped limp at his side. He and his men realized that they were dealing with a supernatural power and retreated. As they withdrew, the uncle's arm was healed.

Catarina was soon joined by sixteen other companions, including her and Clare's own mother! Calling themselves the Poor Ladies of San Damiano, with Clare as their superior, the women lived by a strict rule. They owned nothing, went barefoot even in winter, and slept on bare floors. Keeping silent most of the time, they applied themselves to manual labor and prayer. When Clare's father died, she gave her inheritance to the poor, keeping nothing for the Poor Ladies.

"They say that we are too poor, but can a heart which possesses the infinite God be truly called poor?" she once asked.[22]

From time to time, prelates such as Pope Gregory IX tried to impose a less severe rule upon the Poor Ladies of San Damiano, but Clare resisted. She wanted to live only on what the Franciscan friars gave them from their begging. In the end, Pope Gregory, who had defeated some of the world's fiercest rulers, was unable to move the humble Clare of Assisi, and he relented.

Years later, Clare would also stand strong against Saracen troops who were acting under orders of Emperor Frederick II of Sweden.[23] Bands of marauders invaded San Damiano and the cloister, sending the sisters to Clare in terror. Franciscan friar Thomas of Celano, a biographer of St. Francis of Assisi, tells what happened:

> Saint Clare, with a fearless heart, commanded them to lead her, sick as she was, to the enemy, preceded by a silver and ivory case in which the Body of the Saint of saints was kept with great devotion. And prostrating herself before the Lord, she spoke tearfully to her Christ: "Behold, my Lord, is it possible You want to deliver into the hands of pagans Your defenseless handmaids?... I pray You, Lord, protect these Your handmaids whom I cannot now save by myself." Suddenly a voice like that of a child resounded in her ears from the tabernacle: *"I will always protect you!"* "My Lord," she added, "if it is Your wish, protect also this city which is sustained by Your love." Christ replied, *"It will have to undergo trials, but it will be defended by My protection."* Then the virgin, raising a face bathed in tears, comforted the sisters: "I assure you, daughters, that you will suffer no evil; only have faith in Christ." Upon seeing the courage of the sisters, the Saracens took flight and fled back over the walls they had scaled, unnerved by the strength of she who prayed.[24]

This was not the only miracle for which Clare became known throughout Europe. Toward the end of her life, she was confined to bed on Christmas Eve and longed to attend Mass at the church. The Lord favored her with a vision of the Mass, which played out upon the wall of her room. She was later able to name all the friars who had attended. Seven hundred years later, this miracle inspired Pope Pius XII to name her the patron saint of television.

St. Clare ruled over her order for forty-two years, and her reputation for holiness and fantastic miracles spread throughout Europe. She was fifty-nine years old when she died. Pope Innocent IV assisted at her funeral, and only upon the advice of his cardinals did he refrain from canonizing her on the same day. His successor, Pope Alexander IV, would do so two years later.

Ten years after her death, Pope Urban IV officially named Clare's order the Order of St. Clare or Poor Clares. St. Clare's witness shows us that nothing is impossible for God.

St. Clare of Assisi, woman of courage and strength, pray for us.

SAINTLY TAKEAWAY: St. Clare's faith in God sustained her in all things. How has your faith in God sustained you?

A Rosary Story
Learning Christ
DIANE BATES

I was blessed to be born a Catholic. Unfortunately, like many cradle Catholics, I fell away from the Church in college. When I returned to the faith in my thirties, I began to pray the Rosary again. It was my "prayer of petition." I prayed every Rosary for something or someone, and I saw amazing results.

Then, in 2002, I read Pope St. John Paul II's apostolic letter on the Rosary, *Rosarium Virginis Mariae*. In it, he explains that we should pray the Rosary as a meditation with Mary. We should allow her to teach us about her Son.

> It is not just a question of learning what he taught but of *"learning him."* In this regard could we have any better teacher than Mary?... Among creatures no one knows Christ better than Mary; no one can introduce us to a profound knowledge of his mystery better than his Mother. (*RVM*, 14)

This gave me a new perspective on the Rosary. I found that the more I let Mary teach me, the more deeply I fell into each mystery. I began to experience the joy, illumination, sorrow, and glory of Our Lord through the maternal eyes of the Blessed Mother.

For example, one day while praying the mystery of the Nativity, I felt the Blessed Mother showing me that all of creation was represented at the Nativity scene. The star represented the heavens, the angel represented celestial beings, the straw represented the plant kingdom, and the animals represented the animal kingdom. The Magi represented the gentiles and the rich, while the shepherds represented the Jews and the poor. I was swept up in the majesty of this mystery: *All* creation pays homage to Our Lord.

Over the years, these meditations with Our Lady have been a tremendous blessing to me. I still petition the Lord through the Rosary, but I do it in the midst of awe and wonder. The Rosary not only transforms the people and situations that I pray for but transforms me too!

Thank you, Blessed Mother, for your maternal intercession and maternal formation through the most holy Rosary!

Diane Bates, PhD, is the wife of Deacon Tom Bates, a mother, a grandmother, and a member of the Central Service Team of Magnificat, a worldwide ministry to Catholic women.

Chapter Nine

Your Special Forces Team

WARRIOR HEROES OF RECENT TIMES

Wise warriors are mightier than strong ones,
and those who have knowledge than those
who have strength;
for by wise guidance you can wage your war,
and in abundance of counselors there is victory.
—PROVERBS 24:5–6, NRSV

In every day and time, in every era and century, God determines that there shall be those who present his face to the world. They often come from humble origins, sometimes rejected by others, oftentimes overlooked so unassuming are they, and occasionally reviled because of what they have to say. These men and women are qualitatively different from the rest. Something is transmitted through them—a power, a light, a fire, something of the God-life itself. And it sets off shock waves in the world of man, bringing transformation and renewal, hope and healing, new life.

Recall the words of St. Louis de Montfort about the great saints we can expect in the latter days:

> These great souls, full of grace and zeal, shall be chosen to match themselves against the enemies of God, who shall rage on all sides,... and they shall be singularly devout to our Blessed Lady, illuminated by her light, strengthened with her nourishment, led by her spirit, supported by her arm and sheltered under her protection, so that they shall fight with one hand and build with the other.[1]

The saint goes on:

> They shall be the ministers of the Lord who, like a burning fire, shall kindle the fire of divine love everywhere.... They shall be clouds thundering and flying through the air at the least breath of the Holy Ghost.... They shall thunder against sin; they shall storm against the world; they shall strike the devil and his crew; and they shall pierce through and through, for life or for death, with their two-edged sword of the Word of God (Ephesians 6:17), all those to whom they shall be sent on the part of the Most High.[2]

These prophetic words beg us to consider how godless the last days will be, such that they will require such profound provision from heaven. While many prior generations of man could have said that their time was perhaps the time St. Louis describes, we must ask if these words hold a particular reference to our time.

Perhaps Pope Benedict XVI gives us a hint to the answer when he writes to the bishops of the Church about the state of the world:

> In our days, when in vast areas of the world the faith is in danger of dying out like a flame which no longer has fuel, the overriding priority is to make God present in this world and to show men and women the way to God. Not just any god, but the God who spoke on Sinai; to that God whose face we recognize in a love which presses "to the end" (see John 13:1)—in Jesus Christ, crucified and risen. The real problem at this moment of our history is that God is disappearing from the human horizon, and, with the dimming of the light which comes from God, humanity is losing its bearings, with increasingly evident destructive effects.[3]

These words certainly suggest that we may have arrived at the time prophesied by St. Louis de Montfort. They paint a distressing picture of our current situation and portend an even worse reality to come.

Who then has made the face of God present in the recent past? Who has communicated to us a power, a light, a fire—something of the God-life itself—that shows us the way to transformation and renewal, hope and healing, new life? Let's meet a few.

St. José Sánchez del Río, Viva Cristo Rey
(1913–1928)

Patron for protection of the Eucharist

FEAST DAY: FEBRUARY 10

"Viva Cristo Rey y Santa Maria de Guadalupe!"

Since the earliest days of the Church, her strongest warriors have been formed in the crucible of fiercest strife, from the bloody persecutions of Nero and Diocletian to the murderous rampages of Hitler and Stalin. These times, along with their incumbent evils that so sorely tested the hearts of man, were the times of saint making.

Such was the case of a fourteen-year-old Mexican boy named José Sánchez del Rio. He grew up in the central-western Mexican states, during a time when the faithful were suffering severe oppression caused by anti-Catholic, anticlerical policies of the Mexican government. President Plutarco Elías Calles, whom some labeled a Communist, signed into law a virulent enforcement of the restrictions against the Catholic Church that the Mexican Constitution of 1917 had put forth. The "Calles Law" sought to eliminate the power of the Catholic Church and all organizations affiliated with it, even stamping out popular devotions and religious celebrations in local communities.

Government forces went on a rampage, murdering priests and razing churches throughout the country. But Calles underestimated the tenacity of committed Catholics, who knew full well that "he who is in you is greater than he who is in the world" (1 John 4:4). A massive uprising of the faithful sprang up against Calles. Fueled by prayer and the sacraments, they called themselves the Cristeros, and they used as their rallying cry "*Viva Cristo Rey y Santa Maria de Guadalupe!*" or "Long live Christ the King and Our Lady of Guadalupe!"

Such was the state of the Mexican world when young José Sánchez del Rio was coming of age. Witnesses of his life speak of him as a normal child, much like other children. He went to school, played with his companions, and loved his parents and his relatives. He prayed the Rosary with his parents and attended Mass at the parish of St. James in Sahuayo, Michoacán, where he was baptized and confirmed and received his First Communion. Little could anyone have known that in the not-too-distant future, he would be held captive and tortured in that very church by federal soldiers and then be martyred.

As a young teenager, this boy wanted nothing more than to join his two older brothers on the battlefield. His fervor to fight was surpassed only by his great devotion to the Blessed Sacrament and the Virgin of Guadalupe. He could not bear the sight and sound of the blasphemies being hurled against Our Lord. He pleaded with his mother to let him join the Cristeros.

"In order to go to Heaven, we have to go to war!" he told her.

"You cannot go, you are too young!" she objected.

"Mama, do not let me lose the opportunity to gain Heaven so easily and so soon," he argued.[4]

In 1927, José wrote a letter to Cristero general Prudencio Mendoza, requesting permission to fight. The general acquiesced, as did José's mother, and General Mendoza assigned José to work in the camp. His duties included cleaning and feeding the horses and baking beans for the soldiers. In the evenings, he led the men in praying the Rosary. He soon won the admiration and respect of all those in the Cristero camp, and he ascended to the rank of "Ensign" or flag bearer.

But José would not be on the battlefield for long. On February 5, 1928, he was captured during a battle and imprisoned in a church sacristy. His captors terrorized him by forcing him to watch the hanging of other captives. José encouraged one condemned prisoner to stand strong for Christ: "You will be in Heaven before me. Prepare a place for me. Tell Christ the King I shall be with him soon."[5]

On February 8, just three days after his capture, José was transferred to his hometown of Sahuayo, Michoacán. There he was held prisoner in the baptistery of St. James parish, which the federal soldiers were using as a prison and a stable for their animals. Through the window of the baptistery, friends and family passed fruits and breads with Holy Communion smuggled within.

One night, José heard the crowing of the prize-fighting roosters that belonged to one of the federal officials. He managed to untie himself and discovered that the roosters were tied to the altar in the sanctuary. Filled with holy zeal against such profanity, he wrung the necks of every one of them. The next morning, when the official found out what he had done, he threatened to kill José.

Two days later, his captors turned their ferocity on José, torturing him by shearing the skin off the soles of his feet and forcing him to walk on salt. Even though he screamed in pain, he refused to renounce Christ. His soul remained strong, fortified in the graces of his confirmation, which lent him "a special strength of the Holy Spirit to spread and defend the faith by word and action" (*CCC*, 1303), even in the face of the demonic hatred of his enemies.

Regardless of the torments they inflicted upon him, José would not capitulate. Relying upon the grace of God received via the sacraments, he held his head high as he was marched to a local cemetery. His captors once again demanded, "If you shout, 'Death to Christ the King,' we will spare your life." José flatly refused. Instead he shouted, "Long live Christ the King! Long live Our Lady of Guadalupe!"

Infuriated by his fortitude, the leader of the group demanded that he be killed. "Bayonet him to death," he ordered. As each brutal stab pierced his body, José continued to give witness, *"Viva Cristo Rey!"* Finally, the leader pulled out a pistol and shot him.

On November 20, 2005, Pope Benedict XVI declared José Sánchez del Rio a martyr and raised him to the altar as Blessed. Eleven years later, on October 16, 2016, Pope Francis canonized him along with six others. Saint José Sánchez del Rio shows us that youth is no obstacle to heroic courage and love of God.

St. José Sánchez del Rio, brave warrior for Christ, pray for us.

SAINTLY TAKEAWAY: "And a little child shall lead them" (Isaiah 11:6). Looking back at St. José's biography, in what ways does he exemplify this passage? In what specific ways might he lead you today?

St. Maximilian Kolbe, Our Lady's Public Agent (1894–1941)

Patron of the news media and pro-life movement
FEAST DAY: AUGUST 14

"I would like to be ground to dust for the Immaculate Virgin and have the dust be blown away by the wind all over the world."[6]
—ST. MAXIMILIAN KOLBE

Here is a man known for his great charity and indefatigability. Yet there are two traits that distinguish the admirable St. Maximilian Kolbe more than these: his utter devotion to the Blessed Virgin Mary and his warrior spirit to defend her and the Holy Catholic Church.

Born Raymond Kolbe on January 8, 1894, in the small Polish town of Zdunska Wola, he was raised in a home full of ardent Catholics. Their faith was centered on Mary, the Queen of Poland and especially Our Lady of Czestochowa. It was a fierce, confident, and even somewhat militant faith. This was the foundation upon which Julius Kolbe and his wife, Maria Dabrowska, built their humble but happy home life.

Francis was the only child being groomed for school. But that changed one day, when Raymond went to pick up a prescription and used its Latin name. Impressed, the pharmacist offered to tutor him gratis so he could start school the next year with his brother.

When both boys entered school, they had already developed an interest in joining the Conventual Order of Franciscans, and they were considered ideal candidates. They were soon living at the Franciscan school in L'viv where they received free room, board, and tuition.

While the whole Kolbe family was pious, Raymond was especially fervent, mostly due to a vision of the Blessed Virgin that he had in his youth. The only one he told about the vision was his mother. It had occurred one day after he and his friends were acting wild, and his mother said, "My little son, I don't know what's going to become of you."

Raymond was struck by the comment, and later he prayed to the Blessed Mother, to ask what would become of him. She appeared holding two crowns, one white and the other red, and she asked him if he would accept either one. The white meant that he would persevere in purity, and the red that he would become a martyr. Raymond chose both. From that day on, his mother said, he was so different that she became certain he would die a martyr.

Raymond entered the Franciscan seminary, where he quickly distinguished himself as a brilliant student and a man on fire for God. He had a way of combining piety with a fascination for the new communication technologies of the time, which he believed could help evangelize the world. He dreamed of how to use cinema, radio, and publishing to spread the faith.

But first he had to complete his education, for which he was sent to Rome. In between the completion of a doctorate in philosophy from Gregorian University and another doctorate from the Franciscan International College, on April 28, 1918, Raymond was ordained. He would forevermore be known as Fr. Maximilian.

Only one shadow fell upon those happy years in Rome. One time he spit up blood during a school soccer match. He had tuberculosis, a disease that would plague him for the rest of his life.

But no disease, regardless of how vicious, could check the drive within Fr. Maximilian to serve God through the Immaculate Heart of his mother. During his stay in Rome, he founded the Militia Immaculatae, the Army of Mary Immaculate. It was January 20, 1917, and the Catholic world was celebrating the seventy-fifth anniversary of the apparitions at Lourdes. The mission of the apostolate was evangelization under the guidance of Mary as the Immaculate Mother of Christ. The group started with only six members.

Fr. Maximilian returned to Poland, became a professor of Church history at the seminary, and sought additional ways to use his talents and energy for the sake of the Gospel. He wanted to flood the earth "with a mighty deluge of Christian and Marian literature" in various languages, to drown out the errors communicated through the media. He said, "The globe must be encircled by words of life in printed form, so that the world may once again experience the joy of living."[7]

Maximilian was given permission to start a printing company, and he began to beg for the money to launch this new enterprise. In January of 1922, the first issue of *The Knight of the Immaculate* came out, but Maximilian didn't have enough money to publish a second edition. After announcing this to his readership, he went before a statue of Mary and prayed for help. Later, when he returned for more prayer, he found an envelope on the altar with the exact amount of money he needed. It was addressed: "For you, my Immaculate Mother."[8] Within two years, Fr. Maximilian had distributed five thousand copies of *The Knight*.

The priest eventually bought his own press, a rickety old machine. His labors were not in vain. By 1936, *The Knight* had a circulation of eight hundred thousand. While this number was amazing, it was only a harbinger of what was to come. By the time the Nazis rose to power, Maximilian was printing 800,000 copies a month of *The Knight*, 170,000 copies of *Young Knight*, and 30,000 copies of *Little Knight*. He was also sending out 15,000 copies of a quarterly in Latin for priests and 135,000 copies of a daily Catholic newspaper.

These efforts eventually brought in enough money to buy a more modern press. This led to the acquisition of land and the building of a larger facility, where Maximilian could realize yet another dream, a "City of the Immaculata." Here he built a new Conventual Franciscan monastery, which became a major religious publishing center, followed by a junior seminary two years later.

Throughout this hectic time in his life, Maximilian dealt with several life-threatening flare-ups of tuberculosis, which forced him to retire for weeks at a time. But his thirst for

souls would not let him rest for long. Soon he was establishing another "City of the Immaculata" in Japan. Armed
with all the power of heaven, he built a new publishing enterprise on the slope of Mount Hikosan, which faced away from
the city of Nagasaki. The location of this building, as incon-
venient as it was at the time, would save it on the day in 1945
when the atomic bomb was dropped. The building and all the
people within it would survive with only minor damage. (We
told this amazing story in chapter one.)

Maximilian wanted to do even more for his benevolent Mother. He obtained permission from his superiors to
erect similar establishments in other parts of the world. And
in 1938, on the Feast of the Immaculate Conception, he
launched a radio station.

This was as far as Fr. Maximilian would go in this life. Poor
health forced him back to Poland, where he returned to his
original City of the Immaculata. As the Nazis approached
the area, he dispersed his workers, while he remained in the
monastery with a few other priests. On September 19, 1939,
they were arrested and taken to Amtitz concentration camp,
then mysteriously released on the Feast of the Immaculate
Conception a few months later. Fr. Maximilian told his
companions, "Let us lovingly accept all our crosses, and let
us love every neighbor, whether friend or enemy, without
distinction."[9]

The SS was to visit Maximilian once again, this time to
offer him a chance to escape another trip to the camps. They
offered him German citizenship because he had a German last

name. If he took it, he would be left unharmed. Maximilian refused, which led to his incarceration at Auschwitz.

Even there, the saint's undying love for the faith and the Mother of God made it impossible for him to stay silent. One Holocaust survivor confessed that he had lost his faith because of the evil, but "Kolbe gave that faith back."[10] Another survivor, Alexander Dziuba, said, "When he spoke to us of God, we had the impression that the speaker was someone not of this earth."[11]

Kolbe had but two wishes when he entered Auschwitz. If he had to die, he wanted it to be on a feast of the Blessed Mother, and he wanted to be ground to dust for her, with the dust blown all over the world by the wind. Both desires would be fulfilled.

At the end of July 1941, three prisoners escaped from Auschwitz, which prompted the guards to demand retribution from the prisoners. Ten men were chosen to be starved to death in an underground bunker. When one of the selected men, Franciszek Gajowniczek, cried out, "My wife! My children!" Maximilian immediately spoke up and offered to take his place. The guards allowed it, and the priest was tossed into the bunker along with the other nine men.

Bruno Borgowiec, an assistant to the janitor and also an interpreter at the camp, was an eyewitness of Maximilian's last days on earth.

He recounted that Fr. Kolbe led the prisoners in prayer, in the Rosary, and in songs to the Blessed Mother. So deep in prayer were the poor men that they often were unaware when the SS entered the bunker, until they heard their crude shouts and yelling.

Borgowiec reported that, as the days wore on, the men became weaker, and one by one they died off. Finally, after two weeks, only Fr. Kolbe remained alive. The authorities had more victims to deal with, so they decided to hasten the process. Borgowiec said:

> So one day they brought in the head of the sickquarters, a German, a common criminal named Bock, who gave Fr. Kolbe an injection of carbolic acid in the vein of his left arm. Fr. Kolbe, with a prayer on his lips, himself gave his arm to the executioner. Unable to watch this I left under the pretext of work to be done…. I returned to the cell, where I found Fr. Kolbe leaning in a sitting position against the back wall with his eyes open and his head dropping sideways. His face was calm and radiant.[12]

Deep in the belly of the earth, in a dark dungeon built out of murderous hate, the radiant soul of one of the Church's most glorious saints flew into the arms of heaven.

Never to be outdone in generosity, and no doubt prompted by the desires of his Heavenly Mother, the Lord fulfilled Maximilian's last wishes. On August 15, 1941, the Feast of the Assumption of the Blessed Virgin Mary, his body was placed in the ovens of Auschwitz, and his ashes scattered to the wind.

Fr. Maximilian Kolbe was canonized on October 10, 1982, by Pope St. John Paul II.

St. Maximilian Kolbe, martyr for true charity, pray for us.

SAINTLY TAKEAWAY: St. Maximilian demonstrated heroic virtue at many moments in his life. Which of his virtues do you think is most necessary for you to emulate? Why?

Blessed Mary Restituta Kafka, Witness of the Cross (1894–1943)

Patron for speaking the truth no matter the cost
FEAST DAY: OCTOBER 29
"For the love of God and men."

Known as the only female religious to be formally condemned to death by the Nazis, Blessed Mary Restituta Kafka is the perfect battle partner for those who wish to witness to Christ in the public square.

Born Helena Kafka in the town of Husovice, which is now part of the Czech Republic, on May 1, 1894, she was the sixth daughter of a shoemaker and his wife Maria. Her family moved to a Czech migrant community near Vienna, and it was there she grew up. First a housemaid, then a salesgirl, she became a nurse at the local municipal hospital in 1913. She was hardworking and industrious in all she undertook.

Helena harbored a desire for the religious life, "for the love of God and men," but her parents were against the idea. The matter came to a head when, while working at the hospital, she met the Franciscan Sisters of Christian Charity. A year later, her parents relented. At the age of twenty, Helena entered the order. She was given the name Maria Restituta, after a fourth-century martyr.

Sr. Restituta returned to her work at the hospital. She was transferred in 1919 to Mödling Hospital, where she became the leading surgical nurse. Proficient in her profession, "she soon became an institution in Mödling. Her nursing ability, determination and warmth caused many to call her Sr. Resoluta instead of Sr. Restituta."[13]

The Nazis annexed Austria in 1938 and took over Mödling Hospital. Sr. Restituta did not hide her disdain for the regime. "A Viennese cannot keep her mouth shut," she once said.[14]

When a new hospital wing was constructed, Sr. Restituta made sure that a crucifix was hung in every room. The Nazis later demanded they be taken down, but she refused. Next, they threatened to terminate her employment, but her community complained that they could not replace her. It was a doctor in the hospital, a supporter of the Nazis, who eventually betrayed her to the authorities.

On Ash Wednesday, 1942, as Sr. Restituta was coming out of the operating theater, she was arrested by the Gestapo. The two charges against her were hanging crosses and using "dangerous language," connected with her writing of a poem that mocked Hitler. She spent the next eight months in prison, where she remained openly faithful to both her political and religious beliefs. "I lived for Christ and I'll die for Christ," she said.[15]

On October 29, 1942, Sr. Restituta was sentenced to death by the guillotine for "favoring the enemy and conspiracy to commit high treason." She was offered freedom if she would abandon the Franciscan sisters, but she would not hear of it.

Ranking Nazi officials received requests for clemency for her, but it was determined that her execution would serve as an example for others who might wish to resist the regime.

The last of Sr. Restituta's days were spent caring for other prisoners, many of whom never forgot her almost super-human strength and courage. "She was a saint because in that situation she encouraged everyone, she transmitted a power, a positive spirit and one of confidence," a fellow prisoner recalled.[16]

She exuded that power, confidence, and positive spirit, even in her letters. "No matter how far we are from every-thing, no matter what is taken from us, no one can take from us the faith we have in our heart," she wrote from prison. "In this way we can build an altar in our own heart."[17]

On March 30, 1943, this forty-eight-year-old woman of God was led to the guillotine. She asked a chaplain to make the Sign of the Cross on her forehead just moments before giving her life for Christ. Sr. Restituta was beatified by Pope John Paul II on June 21, 1998.

It's never easy to spread the Gospel of Jesus Christ in secular cultures, and it becomes deadly in countries where govern-ments openly suppress all expressions of faith. Sr. Restituta didn't give her life just for the sake of seeing a crucifix in every room of the hospital. She gave it because of her refusal to let anyone take the cross of Christ out of the world.

"Many things can be taken from us Christians. But we will not let the Cross as a sign of salvation be taken from us," St. John Paul II said during her beatification. "We will not let it be removed from public life! We will listen to the voice of our conscience, which says: 'We must obey God rather than men' (Acts 5:29)."[18]

Blessed Restituta Kafka, courageous woman of grace, pray for us.

SAINTLY TAKEAWAY: How important is the cross of Christ to you? Would you die for the sake of its presence in the world? Ask for the intercession of Blessed Restituta to give you courage and strength to lift high the cross of Christ, that He might draw all to himself (see John 12:32).

Venerable Faustino Pérez-Manglano, a Yes to God (1946–1963)

Postulant of the Marianist Fathers

"I am going to try an asceticism of 'yes' to everything good."

There are four steps in the process of canonization. The second step is the declaration of venerable. At this point, Rome has determined that a candidate has exhibited heroic virtue. And such is the case with this teenage warrior of the faith, whom Pope Benedict XVI declared venerable on January 14, 2011.

Faustino's life began like the lives of so many other saints in the making, without any real distinction or any sign that it would be marked by great sanctity. He led a simple life and a typical one for the boys of his time in Valencia, Spain. He was a soccer fan, a swimmer, and a nature enthusiast.

But by age ten, Faustino clearly showed interests beyond the usual stuff of childhood. He loved Christ and the Blessed

Mother with an intense passion that spilled over into his daily habits and activities. By that young age, Faustino had made a decision to "seek perfection."

The Rosary was at the center of his life of faith, and his custom was to pray it on the way to school every morning. He promised Mary that he would pray the Rosary every day until the year 1961. However, summers, with their outdoor activities, distracted him from his promise, a dilemma he discussed with his spiritual director during his very first retreat at age thirteen.

He told Father José Maria Salaverri that he had kept track of the number of Rosaries he missed through the summers and was trying to catch up and pay back his debt to Our Lady. "How many do you think you missed," the priest gently inquired. Young Faustino replied, "About one hundred." The priest was stunned, not by the number of Rosaries he didn't pray but by his fidelity to keep track of them and by his earnest endeavor to "pay them back."

Wisely, Fr. Salaverri told Faustino that mothers never hold their children to a debt, and he was confident the Blessed Virgin had cancelled his. He told him not to worry about those he missed but just to pray the Rosary as frequently as he could. This Faustino did throughout the rest of his short life.

The next year, Faustino began to keep a diary. He was faithful to it for about a year but added to it only occasionally after that. His initial entries record the ordinary events of his life, while his later missives take on the character of reflections, mostly about his spiritual life.

His first entry, on September 14, 1960, is telling for a couple of reasons: It indicates the beginnings of the disease that would eventually take his life, and it also shows how his faith flowed through his daily living. He wrote, "I got up with the familiar pain. It left me.... I helped Fausto a little with watering. At quarter to nine I prayed the Rosary."

For Faustino, there was no compartmentalizing his relationships with God and with the Blessed Mother. These relationships were as natural to him as the flow of blood through his body.

In November 1960, Faustino became seriously ill. He had cancer from a fatal type of Hodgkin's disease. His suffering was great, made more grueling by the treatment. But he soldiered on without complaint, living a resolution he had made while on retreat: "I am going to try an asceticism of 'yes' to everything good."

In January of 1961, Faustino wrote, "I am still ill and I don't know when I will be able to go to school.... Even though it costs me a lot to pray, I pray the Rosary every day, except a few days that I missed."

By this time, Faustino had begun to discern a call to religious life and to the priesthood. His diary makes mention of this vocation from time to time, and he seemed convinced this was God's plan for him. He was an aspirant to the Marianists, a decision that brought him great joy and spiritual growth. That, coupled with his discovery of the value of redemptive suffering, was leading him to sanctity.

This is seen in his diary entries from November 1960 to May 1961. While they record his pain and suffering, their spiritual quality is undeniable. They reflect a deep interior life and a great love of Jesus and his mother:

> Every day I love Mary more. She is my Mother.... Jesus, let me love Mary,... because she is Your mother and You love her infinitely.... If I want to imitate Christ, my Master, I must do it by infinitely loving what he infinitely loves, His Mother and mine.[19]

Faustino's health improved, and his parents took him to two Marian sites in Europe, one of which was Lourdes, France. He wrote in his diary about his experience there. This visit made a profound impression upon him, especially because of the charity the sick had for each other.

Faustino's health would hold until the fall of 1962. No treatment was helping him, but he was determined to complete his final year of school. He was so frail that his mother had to dress him in the mornings, and he could only make it through half the day. By January of 1963, the cancer was in full force. Somehow, though, he made his annual retreat at the end of the month. In his retreat notes, he reflects on death:

> We must accept death as of now. A death with the Virgin is marvelous. Christ, grant that every day I might be more devoted to Mary. I want to be always intimately united to her. She will help me to die, and I will have the death of a true saint. Let death come when God wants and where God wants. It will come at the time, the place, and in the way that is best for me, sent by Our Father, God. Welcome to our sister, death.[20]

Faustino's health rapidly declined after the retreat. His spiritual director visited him regularly. On March 3, Fr. Salaverri came to give him good news. The next day he would receive Faustino's vows as a Marianist. A special consideration had been obtained, given the circumstances.

At eleven o'clock that night, Faustino asked his mother for a drink of water, then told her to go and rest. Shortly thereafter, he called for her help again. And as she held him in her arms, his body took a sudden jolt, and he expired. Indeed, God had chosen the time, the place, and the best way for Faustino to die—cradled in his mother's warm embrace. In a scene reminiscent of one that took place on a hill outside of Jerusalem over two thousand years ago, Faustino's soul journeyed from one maternal set of arms to another. He was off to greet the heavenly Mother to whom he was dedicated.

According to his spiritual director, at the heart of Faustino's holy life was the recitation of the Rosary. His cause for canonization remains active. Let us seek his intercession.

Venerable Faustino Pérez-Manglano, a true son of Mary, pray for us.

SAINTLY TAKEAWAY: Unlike our other saints, Faustino's courage was not proven through missionary activity, military engagement, or facing flesh-and-blood enemies. Rather, his was a soldierly quest for perfection, a commitment to prayer, and devotion to Christ and His Mother. And when disease ravaged his young body, it included an earnest conformity to the will of God in all things. Which of these strikes you most deeply, and why?

A Rosary Story

One More Day of Rosaries

DAVID CALVILLO

"The Rosary is for old ladies and funerals. I am a man. The Rosary is not for me."

I was one of those ignorant knuckleheads who believed that. I should have known better. My saintly mother always tried to teach her eldest son that devotion to Our Blessed Mother and the power of the Rosary were gifts that could lead me down the best path for life. But alas, I was too blinded by testosterone or vanity or society's norms to realize that Mom knew best.

Then the Holy Spirit led me to an ACTS retreat (see actsmissions.org), where the power of the Rosary and St. Louis de Montfort's spirituality were revealed to me in a visceral way. In response to the joy of that retreat, my wife and I formed Real Men Pray the Rosary, an apostolate to speak to men like me and to all Christians about the power of this beautiful prayer.

A year or two later, my mom (I liked to call her my "Mother Dear") was at death's doorstep after a massive heart attack. The physician predicted death that very day. I refused to leave Mother Dear's side. Joined by one of my beloved aunts, I prayed Rosary after Rosary in that hospital room, through the night and into the next day.

When my pastor arrived to administer the last rites, he instinctively reached into his bag and said, "We have to pray the Rosary." He must have known by my smile how I'd spent the last twenty-four hours or so. He paused and said, "Well, let's pray it again." And so we did. Then Fr. Alfonso said, "We are now going to pray the Litany of the Saints so that the saints can be there to welcome and comfort your mother."

I had never heard of the Litany of the Saints, but as we invoked the roster of names, I smiled, knowing in my heart that Mother Dear would love to be welcomed by Our Blessed Mother and this community of saints. Mother Dear was, after all, our very own living Catholic encyclopedia, who could instantly recite the patron saint of this cause or that condition. I found the litany very comforting.

In an hour or two, as my dad, all of my siblings and their spouses, and my mom's sisters knelt in prayer around her bed, my mother passed. A faithful Filipino nurse attending to us looked at me and said, "This would be a good time to pray the Divine Mercy Chaplet." And so we did. Within moments of concluding that beautiful prayer, I realized that Mother Dear had hung on to life for one last twenty-four-hour period so that she could send a clear message to this son.

Mother Dear passed away on April 28, the Feast of St. Louis de Montfort, the apostle of the Rosary and of total consecration to Jesus through Mary. The message to me was clear: My Mother Dear and Our Blessed Mother approved of the work of Real Men Pray the Rosary, Inc.

Totus Tuus!

David and Valerie Calvillo, the cofounders of Real Men Pray the Rosary, Inc., have eight children and live in Texas. David is the author of Real Men Pray the Rosary: A Practical Guide to a Powerful Prayer.

Chapter Ten

Our Lady's Militia Today

A Call to the Church Militant

In the Heavens Mary commands the Angels and the
blessed.... God has empowered her and commis-
sioned her to fill with saints the empty thrones from
which the apostate angels fell. [1]

—St. Louis de Montfort

We have just met some of the saints of heaven whose
lives demonstrate the capacity to do great things for
God through the intercession of Our Blessed Virgin Mary.
And we have seen how the Rosary was for many of them their
prayer weapon of choice. We learned how it protected them
from hostile actions and attacks. We saw how it inspired them

to stand firm, steadfast, and resolute in the face of imprison-
ment, persecution, and death. We also saw how the prayer of
the Rosary encouraged and increased their faith, hope, and
love in the midst of life's vicissitudes, aiding them in their
struggle to be conduits of God's omnipotence and channels
of his redemptive grace. For them, the Rosary was the spiritual weapon that obtained the victory—if not in this life, then
certainly in the next.

Would we dare, then, to deny the power of the Rosary in
this moment of man's history? Or would we, rather, seek to
make use of it with confidence, courage, and consistency? If
we choose the latter, we may well be on our way to becoming
the great saints prophesied by St. Louis de Montfort, who,
under Our Lady's banner, will bring about great victories for
the Kingdom of Heaven in this moment of history.

MARY'S WARNING

Fraught as our day and time is with such unprecedented challenges the prayer of the Rosary is essential. Recall the prophetic
words of St. John Paul II that we quoted in chapter one:

> We are now standing in the face of the greatest historical
> confrontation humanity has gone through.... We are now
> facing the final confrontation between the Church and the
> anti-church, between the Gospel and the anti-gospel.[2]

If the confrontation was being "faced" in 1976, it has certainly
been engaged in these intervening decades. We have watched
Western civilization crumble as secular humanism and relativism have pummeled its foundations, attacking objective

truth and moral certitude along with it.

All of this leads us to wonder if our current cultural climate could be the frightening fulfillment of the prophecy given by the Blessed Mother at Fatima? Recall that she told the three shepherd children that if her requests were heeded, Russia would be converted, and there would be peace. But if her requests were not heeded, Russia would "spread her errors throughout the world, causing wars and persecutions against the Church." Our Lady said the good would "be martyred," the Holy Father would have much to suffer, and various nations would be annihilated.

And don't we know the history? People continued to offend God. Peace was not attained. And the "worse war" that Our Lady predicted came. World War II broke out under the pontificate of Pope Pius XII, and it was far more devastating than World War I, with direct deaths three times greater. While the Second World War saw the defeat of the Third Reich, atheistic Communism continued its march, controlling whole nations under its ideologies. Nations were annihilated, and countries buckled under the red star's quest for world domination.

Even when the Cold War came to an end on the Feast of the Immaculate Conception, December 8, 1991, with the defeat of the Soviet Union, Russia's errors continued to proliferate. Certainly this is true in the political sense, since varieties of communism still control governments throughout the world. But the errors have spread in other ways as well.

Atheistic Marxist ideologies have wormed their way into the social policies, economics, and agendas of the West.

They have come by way of academia, left-leaning politicians, misguided clerics, legislation, government-run elementary and high schools, and the ubiquitous power of the media.[3] So ingrained have the tenets of socialism become that they may well be the prevailing shaper of the contemporary mind-set. It is a new kind of totalitarianism—a cultural totalitarianism—that heralds, if not in words then most definitely in practice, "God is dead."

As Joseph Cardinal Ratzinger writes in *Faith and the Future*:

> The man of today [holds as] his slogan…"Progress", not "Tradition"; "Hope", not "Faith."… For that to which he looks forward is not, as in the early Church, the kingdom of God, but the kingdom of man, not the return of the Son of Man, but the final victory of a rational, free, and brotherly order among men who have discovered *themselves*.… Thus, for the man of today hope no longer means looking for things over which we have no control, but action by our own power. Man expects redemption to come from himself.[4]

OUR MISSION

So what does this mean for us and for future generations? Are we doomed to a civilization structured according to the erroneous ideologies of the prevailing demagogue? Or a political system that creates a "nanny state" by pandering to the passions of the populace at the expense of true human flourishing? Or a legal system that muzzles religious expression in the public square, substituting freedom of worship for freedom of religion? Or a culture that breeds contempt for people of faith by stereotyping, marginalizing, vilifying, and criminalizing them?

We are doomed only if we let ourselves be. As the centuries-old saying goes, "The only thing necessary for the triumph of evil is for good men to do nothing."[5]

The responsibility to preserve and protect that which is God-honoring, and to reclaim that which is lost, always belongs to the believer. Consider these words from 2 Chronicles 7:14: "If *my* people who are called by my name humble themselves, and pray and seek my face, and turn from their wicked ways, then I will hear from heaven, and will forgive their sin and heal their land" (emphasis added).

This, then, is our call and mission, as the people of God to whom he has given life in this moment in the history of man. And isn't this what the Blessed Virgin Mary told us at Fatima and in all of her apparitions? We are called to pray, to make sacrifices, to repent, and to move forward under her motherly protection. And when we commend ourselves to her, the "Holy Spirit communicates Himself to that soul abundantly" and does startling wonders through her.[6]

MORE FORCES FOR THE BATTLE

Our Lady, Queen of the Angels, dispatches the angelic forces to our service. She "is the general of the armies of God and the angels form the glorious troops; thus they are the soldiers of her who alone is terrible as a whole army in battle array."[7]

According to Henri Marie Boudon, the great Catholic priest and spiritual writer, the angels are fiercely devoted to Mary. "They are...her servants," he writes, "but such zealous servants that they await but the manifestation of her will to execute it, at its least sign, with a promptitude that is indescribable."[8] She is their commander, says St. Louis de Montfort, "the likes of which are beyond the imagination of men."[9]

And her command over the angels is one more reason why the powerful "woman" of Genesis has always been considered Satan's most formidable enemy. "Men do not fear a powerful, hostile army as much as the powers of hell fear the name and protection of Mary," St. Bonaventure wrote.[10]

Centuries later, St. Louis de Montfort expressed something similar:

> God has fashioned and shaped only one enmity, and that an irreconcilable one, which will endure and even increase, until the end. It is that between the Virgin Mary and the Devil, between the children and servants of the Blessed Virgin and the children and accomplices of Satan; so that the most terrible of the enemies of Satan created by God is Mary, his Blessed Mother.[11]

St. Louis tells us that Mary will always have the victory over that proud spirit. She will always discover his evil intention and "lay bare his infernal plots and dissipate his diabolical councils, and even to the end of time will guard her faithful servants from his cruel claw."[12] Mary's motherly beatitude, encompassing protection, and her profound intercession will always be with us. She will crush the serpent's head with her little heel—her "humble slaves and her poor children, whom she will raise up to make war against him," and who will "carry on their shoulders the bloody standard of the Cross, the Crucifix in their right hand and the Rosary in their left, the sacred Names of Jesus and Mary in their hearts, and the modesty and mortification of Jesus Christ in their own behavior."[13]

A CALL TO ACTION: A BATTLE PLAN FOR OUR DAY AND TIME

To be sure, when we pray the Rosary in our personal time of prayer with intentionality and devotion, asking Our Lady to take us into the mysteries of her Son's life even as we pray for those mysteries to come to life in us, great grace is merited for us. As we have discovered, a process of on-going transformation takes place in our soul by means of the divine life those mysteries hold. As the Eastern Fathers of the Church tell us, we become "divinized," "deified," ever more conformed to the Word Made Flesh. Thus, our intercession becomes purer, more Christlike, more in union with the intercession of Our Lord and Savior. And this makes it more powerful and efficacious.

So, too, is it when we pray the Rosary with others. In union with other brothers and sisters in the faith, the transforming dynamic of the Rosary unites all of us in Christ's prayer of intercession that forever ascends to the throne of the Father and our prayer becomes mystically caught up in his. Remember that Jesus tells His apostles, "Again, truly I tell you, if two of you agree on earth about anything you ask, it will be done for you by my Father in heaven. For where two or three are gathered in my name, I am there among them" (Matthew 18:19–20).

Recall the amazing victory won at Lepanto through the corporate praying of the Rosary by the faithful gathered together in Churches throughout Europe as the battle raged. And recall as well the victory won in Brazil as the women came together in both small groups and mass demonstrations to pray the Rosary. The Communists' planned takeover of their country was foiled as holy hands plied holy beads in supplication for Heaven's intervention.

Are we ready to pick up our holy weapon, the Rosary, and stand with Our Lady for all that gives glory to God? To suffer persecution in union with Christ, should circumstances require it, in reparation for our sins and the sins of the world? Are we willing to pray for the grace of final perseverance and to pray for the desire to receive the red rose of martyrdom if God so wills? If so, then let's invoke the intercession of Our Blessed Lady under her title Queen of Angels and set out under her holy standard with her Rosary in our hand.

The Warrior's Rosary Crusade

Following is an eight-step plan to execute a Warrior's Rosary Crusade in your parish, community, or locale. Additionally, you will find a description of a uniquely designed Rosary perfectly suited for just such a campaign. Called "The Warrior's Rosary," it captures in its crucifix, centerpiece, and

Our Father medals, the power of the Rosary as a weapon for spiritual warfare. In chapter eleven, you will find meditations for the spiritual battle, and in chapter twelve you will find tips on praying your Rosary with greater intentionality and effect.

A Call to "Arms:" Your Battle Plan

The witness of Doña Amelia Bastos provides us with excellent insight on how to begin and lead an effective Rosary Crusade. Most of the eight steps are adapted from the plan she followed in Brazil:

Step One: Gather together family and friends, colleagues and parishioners to talk about the reality of spiritual warfare and how it affects our lives personally and corporately. Two resources are of particular value: this book, *The Rosary: Your Weapon for Spiritual Warfare*, and a DVD presentation by Thomas K. Sullivan called *Our Lady in God's Plan for the Kingdom*. Information on ordering these resources, as well as a Warrior's Rosary, is available for you at www.womenofgrace.com.

Step Two: Encourage those who gather to form a Warrior Rosary Crusade prayer group in their home or at their parish.

Step Three: Start your own Warrior Rosary Crusade prayer group in your home or parish by inviting ten friends. Pray the Rosary together as a group using the meditations in chapter eleven. Meet once a week to pray the Rosary for the challenges of our day and time and to discuss the content of this book on a chapter-to-chapter basis if desired. If your group is meeting in a parish setting, ask participants to invite someone new to join them each week.

Step Four: Encourage participants to "pass it on" by starting a Warrior Rosary Crusade prayer group in their own homes.

Step Five: Distribute information about the Rosary and the Warrior's Rosary to family, friends and, with the pastor's approval, parishioners.

Step Six: With your pastor's permission, plan a Rosary procession for your parish and invite family, friends, relatives, and parishioners to attend. A feast day of the Blessed Mother is always an appropriate date for such a devotional practice.

Step Seven: Familiarize yourself and others about the plenary indulgence that may be gained by praying the Rosary under the following conditions:

- The Rosary may be offered individually or as a group in a church, family group, or religious community.
- All five decades must be prayed continuously and vocally, while meditating on the mysteries. If the recitation of the Rosary is public, the mysteries of the Rosary must be announced.
- To obtain a plenary indulgence, three other conditions must be met: making a sacramental confession, receiving Eucharistic Communion, and offering prayers for the pope's intentions.
- One must be free of all attachments to sin, even venial sin, to obtain a full plenary indulgence. If this integrity is not present or if the other conditions are not met, the indulgence is only partial.

- A plenary indulgence may be gained only once each day, except by those in danger of death. Both plenary and partial indulgences may be applied to the dead.[14]

Step Eight: Be a Rosary evangelizer! Make use of every opportunity Our Lord presents to share the power of the Rosary.

THE WARRIOR'S ROSARY: A ONE-OF-A-KIND SPIRITUAL WEAPON

To illustrate the power of the Rosary, Thomas K. Sullivan has designed the beautiful and distinctive Warrior's Rosary. They come in different styles and colors; one set of these beautiful Rosary beads is featured on this book's cover.

Conceived in prayer and developed over the span of ten years, its unique design unites the realities of spiritual battle and military combat. The Warrior's Rosary reminds us that we are the soldiers of God, chosen for this moment in the history of man, to present His face to the world, as we strive to retain all that is God-honoring in our culture and to reclaim that which has been lost.

Three defining features help to inspire the user of the Warrior Rosary to own the truth of who he is, his mission, and the way he can be an instrument of God at this moment in time.

- **The Crucifix** is a unique representation of three scriptural images: the Word made flesh in the Person of Jesus Christ; the Sword of the Spirit, which is the Word of God; and the cross, by which we attain the gift of salvation. The back of the crucifix reminds the user of the call to be a "soldier of

Christ" (2 Timothy 2:3). It features an image of a sword with the word *KNIGHT* etched on the blade.

• **The Centerpiece Medal** features an image of Our Lady of Mount Carmel holding the Child Jesus, from whom rays of grace rain down. Receiving the grace is a woman knighting a man who kneels before her. The woman represents Holy Mother Church as she administers the sacrament of baptism and the sacrament of confirmation. As Pope Melchiades tells us, "In Baptism man is enlisted into the service, in Confirmation he is equipped for battle."[15]

• **The Our Father Medals** take the places of the beads that divide the decades of most Rosaries. On the Warrior's Rosary, these burnished silver medals are shaped like shields, and each features a warrior saint from one of several geographic locations and time periods. These remind the user of a great truth: No knight or soldier goes into battle alone. These saintly men and women form an elite spiritual "Special Forces Team" to accompany you in battle every time you pray the Rosary. In fact, you have met these saints throughout this book.[16] They are at-the-ready waiting to assist you in spiritual battle and your Warrior Rosary Crusade!

A Rosary Story
Seek First His Kingdom
THOMAS K. SULLIVAN

Growing up, I never thought much about religion, church, or God. Kind of odd, since my mother loved her Catholic faith and made sure all three of us kids went to Mass every Sunday. She even made sure my brother and I were altar boys.

Mom often told us kids about her devotion to the Rosary and Our Lady of Fatima. She marveled at the fact that her Auntie (Tante Lisi) witnessed the miracle of the sun during the final apparition.

But for me, religion was not my thing. It was for women and for people who couldn't make it on their own. Me, I was a risk taker, afraid of nothing, invincible by my own admission. My mother nicknamed me "Tommy Trouble," because if there was danger and excitement, I was in the middle of it.

As a teen, my heart was set on joining the US Navy, and that's what I did at seventeen. Over the next nine years, I advanced through the ranks, conquered new challenges, and received many medals and awards. At age twenty-one, I became one of the youngest persons to be assigned as company commander at Recruit Training Command Orlando, where I spent five years training recruits. During this time, I got married, began a family, and thought I was on top of the world. More proof I didn't need religion. But my life was about to take a radical turn.

In April 1989, I decided to continue my military career with the US Coast Guard. It was good for my young family, because it kept me home on dry land, unlike the Navy. During the transition from one branch to the other, I moved my family in with my parents. It was then that my mother's hours of prayer for me yielded fruit.

Surprisingly, during these few months, I became attracted to the Rosary. I didn't know much about it other than what it was called. I didn't even know the prayers. But I began to experience a desire to have one.

One morning, I asked my mom where she got her religious stuff. She asked me why, and I told her I wanted a Rosary. So off we went. She tried to act calm and matter of fact, but I could see she was ready to explode with joy.

I got the Rosary, and God immediately began to work in me. I'll never forget the following Sunday morning. I was on my parents' back porch when all of a sudden, a warm burning sensation filled my body from head to toe. I felt my heart melt and my legs turn to jelly. In an instant, I knew God was real. The Blessed Mother was also touching my soul, and I knew for a fact she was real too. I knew my life would never be the same. A new path was in front of me, and I was eager to pursue it.

When it was time to go to my duty station, my mother gave me a Bible. On the inside cover, she had inscribed: "Seek ye first the Kingdom of God, and all things shall come to you! Always give God the glory! Mom and Dad."

I am in awe of what God has done over these past decades. Had you told me then that I would go on to author the book *Called to Knighthood: The Sacrament of Confirmation in the Kingdom Family of God*, design the Warrior's Rosary, or coauthor the book you're reading, I would have said you were off your rocker. But all things are possible with God, and to God give all the glory! *Hua!*

Chapter Eleven

The Warrior's Rosary

MEDITATIONS FOR THE BATTLE

Give me an army saying the Rosary
and I will conquer the world.[1]

—POPE PIUS IX

 As we have discovered, the Christian life is a warfare. God has given us powerful spiritual weapons for the battle: Sacred Scripture, the Holy Sacrifice of the Mass, the sacraments, and all of the sacramentals, especially the Rosary.

MEDITATIONS FOR THE BATTLE

Following are meditations to draw us into the mysteries of Christ's life that the Rosary presents. The goal is to consider the great gift of grace given to us in the Rosary to help us meet the struggles of our current time and the trials of our personal lives. We pray that these meditations will encourage you to be a soldier of Christ in this, our day and time, a warrior on the battlefield of life.

As we take up our Rosary beads to pray the Warrior's Rosary, let us open our hearts to the mysteries being presented. Let us seek the intercession of Our Lady to obtain for us the divine favor we need in order to be conformed to the heart of her Son, Jesus Christ.

Begin by offering this Warrior Rosary Reflection on the crucifix:

Father in heaven,
as I prepare to enter into this spiritual battle of prayer,[2]
I take up the weapon of the Rosary.
Holding the crucifix in my hand,
I am reminded of the epic battle your Son fought against
the Evil One and his minions.
I am reminded too that He willingly laid his life down for
me on the Cross and thereby freed me from the bondage
of sin.
As I profess the Apostles' Creed,
I ask for the intercession of the warrior saints and the might
and power of the angelic hosts to aid and assist me now.

Next, recite the Apostles' Creed, Our Father, three Hail Marys, Glory Be, and Fatima Prayer. Now you are ready to pray the mysteries with their corresponding reflections. (More help for praying the Rosary is in chapter twelve.)

THE JOYFUL MYSTERIES (MONDAY, SATURDAY)

The First Joyful Mystery:
The Annunciation of the Angel Gabriel to Mary

The fruit of this mystery is humility.

Father in heaven, I picture the archangel Gabriel coming to announce to Mary that she is to be the Mother of the Messiah. Beholding her, he bends his knee in submission before the woman who is his queen.

"Hail, full of grace, the Lord is with you!" he says (Luke 1:28). "Let it be to me according to your word," she replies (Luke 1:38), and all of heaven erupts with joy. Her *fiat* is her *hua*, and with it, the Word is made flesh and dwells among us. Salvation comes!

Mother, take me into this mystery, and help me to appropriate its grace. May I, like you, give my *fiat* to every request of the Father. Obtain for me the grace of humility to always be at the service of heaven.

Mary, Holy Virgin of Virgins, pray for me.

The Second Joyful Mystery:
The Visitation of Mary to Elizabeth

The fruit of this mystery is charity, love of neighbor.

Father in heaven, as I contemplate this mystery, I am in awe of your providential plan. Even as Mary enters the home of Zachariah and Elizabeth, your Son is about His mission of salvation. John the Baptist gives his *fiat* with a mighty leap in Elizabeth's womb, and Elizabeth confesses with her lips that the child within Mary is her Lord. By bringing her Son to their home, the Woman is already crushing the devil's head.

Like the Blessed Virgin, I too want to be a serpent smiter, a warrior in your kingdom. As I pray this mystery, may my intercession be efficacious in winning souls for you. Our Lady, Queen of Heaven, procure for me the grace to bring Jesus to all whom God entrusts to me, with true charity and love of neighbor.

Mary most amiable, pray for me.

The Third Joyful Mystery:
The Nativity, the Birth of Our Lord Jesus in Bethlehem
The fruit of this mystery is holy detachment and contempt for riches.

Father in heaven, could any life have begun in more lowly estate than that of your Son? What contradiction! The King of Kings is born in a cave, laid in a feeding trough, sung to by animals, and visited by shepherds. And He is the Victor, the Conqueror, the Messiah, the Redeemer!

Help me, in the poverty of my condition, to cooperate with the grace of this mystery, to be more than a conqueror through Christ Jesus by way of Mary's maternal beatitude. Give me contempt for the riches of the world and desire only for the things of God.

Mary, Help of Christians, pray for me.

The Fourth Joyful Mystery:
The Presentation of Jesus in the Temple
The fruit of this mystery is obedience.

Father in heaven, as I contemplate this mystery of your Son's life, I can almost feel the suffering of heart Our Lady experienced. The prophetic word of Simeon must have fallen hard on her ears. Jesus was "set for the fall and rising of many," and a sword would pierce her maternal heart so the secret thoughts of many might be revealed (Luke 2:34–35). Great suffering will accompany her Son's mission and hers in union with it.

I know that I too will not be spared a portion of this passion. It is the way for all soldiers of Christ, for "no slave is greater than his master" (John 15:20, *NAB*). But Christ's Passion, death, and resurrection assure me of victory, of the grace to stand firm against the enemy. May I obediently and joyfully embrace my cross, and may Mary stand with me in all of life's contradictions.

Mary, Tower of David, pray for me.

The Fifth Joyful Mystery:
The Finding of Jesus in the Temple

The fruit of this mystery is piety.

Father in heaven, what fear and anxiety Mary and Joseph must have felt when they realized that their twelve-year-old son was missing! Those three days must have been excruciating! They finally found Him in the temple, about His Father's business (see Luke 2:49). Though joy filled their hearts, the cloud of mystery covered this event.

Mary pondered in her heart. Could she guess that there would be another time when Jesus would be lost to her for three days? She knew triumph in the moment when He was found in the temple. Could she fathom the even greater triumph she would know when her Son rose from the dead?

Mother, pray for me in all of the anxious moments of my life. Obtain for me the gift of piety, to seek God in the midst of my suffering as you did in yours.

Mary, Mother of Divine Grace, pray for me.

THE LUMINOUS MYSTERIES (THURSDAY)

The First Luminous Mystery:
The Baptism of Jesus in the Jordan River
The fruit of this mystery is faithfulness to our
baptismal promises.

Father in heaven, in this most poignant scene of Sacred
Scripture, I discover the institution of the twin sacraments
of baptism and confirmation, and I consider what they mean
for me as a member of the Church Militant. Contrary to the
designs of the Evil One, I am not left orphaned on this battlefield of life. Through these two sacraments, I have received
the graces I need to be amply equipped for spiritual combat.

May the Word of God sustain me, and may I live the grace
of my baptism in and through all things.

Mary, Singular Vessel of Devotion, pray for me.

The Second Luminous Mystery:
The Wedding Feast at Cana
The fruit of this mystery is docility to the will of God.

Father in heaven, I envision the wedding feast in Cana, where
your Son Jesus performs His first miracle. The time for His
mission to be fulfilled has begun, and His mother, Mary,
births Him into it.

"They have no wine," she tells Him. "Woman, what
concern is that to you and to me?'" He asks. Their eyes lock in
a look of eternal knowing. "Do whatever he tells you," Mary
instructs the servants (John 2:3–5, *NRSV*).

Jesus asks them to fill six water jugs. He then changes the
water into wine. Thus does his public ministry begin, and

with it His slow march toward Calvary where evil would be defeated.

Mary, Seat of Wisdom, pray for me.

The Third Luminous Mystery:
The Proclamation of the Kingdom
and the Call to Conversion.

The fruit of this mystery is repentance.

Father in heaven, in this mystery, I hear Jesus preach, "Repent, for the kingdom of heaven is at hand" (Matthew 4:17). I find this a sobering call because of its two commands and the obedience they require.

First, I need to change, to amend my life, to turn from all my wrongdoing, selfishness, and pride. I need to leave behind my desire for earthly gain, pleasure, and status and set my sights on your holy will.

Second, I must recognize who I am in the kingdom family of God and the duty that identity requires. I am a soldier in this kingdom, a knight, and my call is to spread and defend Holy Mother Church. It is for this reason I have been graced through baptism and confirmation, nourished through the Eucharist, and healed through confession.

Lord, give me the grace of docility to the authority you have established in your kingdom. Give me also the grace of repentance when willfulness and stubbornness arise in me.

Mary my mother, Vessel of Honor, pray for me.

The Fourth Luminous Mystery:
The Transfiguration

The fruit of this mystery is the desire for holiness.

Father in heaven, this fourth luminous mystery is both a call and a promise for me. The call is to be so united to Jesus that I too may radiate His love to those around me. You have called me to be a soldier of light in this dark battlefield of the world.

There is also the promise of the rewards that lie ahead, in the resurrection of my body at the end of time. Then I will truly shine with the luminosity of God, for I shall be made holy. I will shine in the likeness of Jesus's resurrected glory.

Father, pour into my heart your Holy Spirit, that this transformation may begin even now. I desire to be the image of Jesus your Son.

Mary, Spiritual Vessel, pray for me.

The Fifth Luminous Mystery:
The Institution of the Eucharist

The fruits of this mystery are Eucharistic Adoration
and active participation at Mass.

Father in heaven, in this mystery, I am transported to the Upper Room. Jesus is there with His twelve apostles. He has charged them to govern his Church, but He is about to honor them with an even greater and more glorious reality. He is going to ordain them into His own divine priesthood and give them the holy privilege of consecration, by which bread and wine become His Body, Blood, soul, and divinity.

What grace is ours! What a gift is the Catholic priesthood! May I never take for granted the Bread from Heaven, nor the holy priests who are *in persona Christi*. May my love for the Eucharistic Presence grow each day!

Mary, Mother of Our Savior, pray for me.

THE SORROWFUL MYSTERIES (TUESDAY, FRIDAY)

The First Sorrowful Mystery:
The Agony in the Garden

The fruit of this mystery is conformity to the will of God.

Father in heaven, as I enter into these sorrowful mysteries, my heart aches for the diabolical suffering your Son endured for me and for all of humanity. The very thought of His temptation in the Garden of Gethsemane reminds me of the temptation in the Garden of Eden, with Satan concealed as a serpent.

While Adam's failure plunged the human race into the abyss of hell's darkness, the victory of Jesus, the New Adam, brings the light of hope and the promise of salvation to all mankind. Through his inaction, Adam surrendered to the Evil One's devilish scheme, while your Son's surrender to your will, Father God, conquered Satan and his diabolic wiles. As I now pray this mystery, I ask you to give me the love and surrender that Jesus displayed. Like Him, may I say, "Not my will but thine be done" (see Matthew 26:39).

Mary, Refuge of Sinners, pray for me.

The Second Sorrowful Mystery:
The Scourging at the Pillar

The fruits of this mystery are purity and mortification.

Father in heaven, what atrocious pain Jesus willingly endured for my sins! With each slap of the whip, His precious flesh was torn from His body, and His holy blood saturated the ground around Him. Such hatred, such fury—surely hell was attacking Him through the Roman soldiers!

Father, help me to always remember the great cost of my salvation, Christ's act of total self-donation on my behalf. How you must love me! Help me to remember this when I am bereft of consolation.

Mary, Comforter of the Afflicted, pray for me.

The Third Sorrowful Mystery:
The Crowning with Thorns

The fruits of this mystery are moral courage and contempt for the world.

Father in heaven, as I meditate on this mystery, I recall how the Roman soldiers mocked your Son, Jesus. They stripped Him of His clothing, gave Him a scarlet robe to wear, and put a reed in His hand. They pushed a thorn branch shaped like a crown onto His head. They knelt before Him, spat upon Him, and laughed at Him with derision and scorn. How hell must have rejoiced! The demons must have clapped their cloven hooves in the air with diabolic glee!

But I have to ask myself, to what extent have I mocked Jesus and His kingship? When I enter into a Catholic Church, do I remember He is present in the tabernacle, Body and Blood, soul and divinity? Do I pay Him homage by genuflecting in acknowledgment of His kingly presence? Am I reverent in all ways? When I approach the altar to receive my Lord in Holy Communion, do I come in a state of grace and with true humility of heart?

Father, strengthen me as a knight in your kingdom, a soldier in the Church Militant. Help me to always be aware of whom it is I serve. May my actions and the disposition of my heart speak to the reality of Jesus Christ, King of Kings, of whom I am but the humble servant.

Mary, Mother of our Creator, pray for me.

The Fourth Sorrowful Mystery:
Jesus Carries His Cross

The fruit of this mystery is patience.

Father in heaven, I mystically journey now with Jesus and His mother along the *Via Dolorosa*. What an excruciating way this is! The weight of the cross bears down upon your Son, and his travail takes its toll. He has been through so much! The cost of his agony, the pain of his scourging, the horror of his crowning and mockery, the loss of blood, and His sheer exhaustion and misery are more than we can imagine. And yet Jesus staggers on, embracing the cross, the instrument of His final torture. He is encouraged and strengthened by His Mother Mary, who accompanies His every step.

Father, may I always realize that no matter how great my suffering, with Jesus I can shoulder my cross. The merits of His sufferings make my yoke easy and my burden light.

Mary, Mother of Christ, pray for me.

The Fifth Sorrowful Mystery:
The Crucifixion of Jesus

The fruits of this mystery are final perseverance,
salvation, and self-denial.

Father in heaven, my soul is pierced with sorrow as I contemplate the crucifixion of your Son. The soldiers hatefully hammered nine-inch nails into His holy hands and feet, impaling Jesus to the cross. They raised it, and for three long hours the King of Kings hung in the scorching sun bearing the entirety of human suffering in His body, soul, and spirit.

But even during his execution, Jesus continued to bring life in abundance. A thief was saved, his mother was bequeathed, John was gifted, and the Church was born. The Evil One thought he had conquered, but when your Son breathed His last, thunder crashed, the lightning cracked, the curtain was rent, and heaven owned the victory.

Father, your Son's sacrifice was for *me*. I am the unworthy recipient of the fruit of Jesus's travail. May I never take this gift lightly, and may I always give glory and praise to you for the gift of everlasting life at the cost of your Son (John 3:16).

Mary, Cause of Our Joy, pray for me.

THE GLORIOUS MYSTERIES (WEDNESDAY, SUNDAY)

The First Glorious Mystery:
The Resurrection

The fruit of this mystery is faith.

Father in heaven, as I reflect on this first glorious mystery, joy and amazement fill my heart! With the resurrection of Jesus, the tables were turned on Satan, his apparent victory foiled. "He is risen. He is risen indeed!" all creation cried.

Father, help me to always be mindful of this great victory won for me by your Son. May I embrace it, live in it, and cherish it until I breathe my last. I look forward to the resurrection of the dead and the life of the world to come. Amen.

Mary, Queen of Martyrs, pray for me.

The Second Glorious Mystery:
The Ascension

The fruits of this mystery are hope and the desire for heaven.

Father in heaven, as I meditate on the ascension of Jesus into heaven, I imagine myself standing there among those to whom He spoke. He told His disciples to stay in the city until they were "clothed with power from on high." And then, leading them out as far as Bethany, He lifted His hands in blessing and "was carried up into heaven" (Luke 24:46–51).

Surely the apostles must have wondered at all they had seen and heard. As they departed, they may well have talked among themselves and puzzled over Our Lord's words. Sometimes I too struggle to understand and am left perplexed. I ask for the grace of the Holy Spirit to illuminate my mind and heart and to give me the virtues of obedience and trust in you.

Mary, Queen of Apostles, pray for me.

The Third Glorious Mystery:
The Descent of the Holy Spirit

The fruits of this mystery are love of God, wisdom, and knowing and sharing the truth.

Father in heaven, the disciples, with the Blessed Virgin Mary and some other holy women, gathered in the Upper Room to prayerfully wait for the descent of the Holy Spirit. Surely Our Lady interceded for her spiritual sons and daughters to be receptive to the gift they were about to receive. As she had given birth to her Son, so too would she now give birth to His Church, His Mystical Body.

And suddenly a sound came from heaven like the rush of a mighty wind.... And there appeared to them tongues as of fire, distributed and resting on each one of them. And they were all filled with the Holy Spirit and began to speak in other tongues, as the Spirit gave them utterance. (Acts 2:2–4)

In an instant, the disciples were transformed! Courage replaced fear; holy zeal replaced timidity. Emboldened, the disciples proclaimed the Gospel message to the multitudes— and three thousand were converted that day.

Father, I ask that you stir up the graces of my baptism and fill me anew with the Holy Spirit. Give me courage and zeal to proclaim the Good News at every opportunity. May my witness yield abundant fruit for the kingdom.

Mary, Virgin Most Venerable, pray for me.

The Fourth Glorious Mystery:
The Assumption of the Blessed Virgin Mary

The fruits of this mystery are devotion to Mary

and the grace of a happy death.

Father in heaven, this holy mystery reminds me that this life is but a pilgrim way and heaven is my real destination. Though Mary's assumption was "a singular participation in her Son's Resurrection," it points to the anticipated resurrection of other Christians as well, including me (*CCC*, 966). I shall rise from the dead and be lifted to the heavenlies when Jesus comes again.

Mary, pray for me, that every choice and decision I make in this life be made with this holy truth in mind. Help me to be faithful to your Son and to His Church. Keep me true to my baptismal promises, and give me strength to live my duty with vigilance, valor, and hope.

Mary, Gate of Heaven, pray for me.

The Fifth Glorious Mystery:
The Coronation of Mary

The fruit of this mystery is eternal happiness.

Father in heaven, utter joy fills me as I contemplate Mary's coronation as Queen of Heaven and Earth. I can only imagine the divine celebration in the heavenlies as your primordial plan was fulfilled! Mary is my queen too, and I desire that she reign in my heart with her Son, Jesus, my Savior and King.

In all ways, Father, help me to be her holy subject, heeding her maternal wisdom and guidance, learning from her as she takes me into the mysteries of her Son's life. Help me to be a valiant knight and rise to her defense, even as I seek to defend Holy Mother Church, of which Mary is the archetype. Blessed Virgin, pray with me that this may be so.

Queen of all Saints, pray for me.

A Rosary Story
Christ to Bishop: Pray the Rosary to Defeat Terrorism
BISHOP OLIVER DASHE DOEME OF NIGERIA,
AS REPORTED BY SUSAN BRINKMANN

On April 21, 2015, Women of Grace staff journalist Susan Brinkmann posted an amazing story in the Breaking News section of our website, womenofgrace.com. A Nigerian bishop claimed to have been told by Christ in a vision that the way to rid his nation of the Islamic terrorist group Boko Haram was to pray the Rosary. Following is the article. It may well come to be known as one of the most important Rosary stories of our time—if we heed its message:

CNA/EWTN News is reporting that Bishop Oliver Dashe Doeme, of the diocese of Maiduguri in the hard-hit Borno state, received a powerful message from Jesus while in prayer. "Toward the end of last year, I was in my chapel before the Blessed Sacrament...praying the Rosary, and then suddenly the Lord appeared," Bishop Dashe told EWTN News April 18.

At first, Jesus said nothing, but He extended a sword toward the bishop, which he reached out to take. "As soon as I received the sword, it turned into a Rosary," the bishop said. According to the bishop, Jesus then told him three times: "Boko Haram is gone."

"I didn't need any prophet to give me the explanation," the bishop said. "It was clear that with the Rosary, we would be able to expel Boko Haram."

At first, the bishop didn't want to tell anyone what had happened, but then he felt that the Holy Spirit was pushing him to do so. He started with the priests of his diocese and then told participants in a conference in Madrid, Spain, which was dedicated to gathering ideas on how to preserve the Christian presence in nations where the faith is the most persecuted.

Bishop Dashe is no stranger to the violence of Boko Haram. His diocese in northeastern Nigeria is in one of the worst-hit areas. It was here that the terrorists seized more than 250 girls from a school in Chibok, most of whom have not been seen again. Just last month, five suicide bombers killed fifty-four people and wounded hundreds in Maiduguri, where the bishop lives. In January, more than 150 people were slaughtered as they tried to flee to safety after the terrorists launched a killing spree in the towns of Baga and Doro Gowon, also located in Borno state. The constant bloodletting has driven thousands of Catholics from their homes. In 2009, there were about 125,000 Catholics in the diocese. That number has now dwindled to about fifty or sixty thousand. Boko Haram has caused the deaths of more than six thousand people since 2009, with more than one thousand killed in just the first three months of 2015.

For now, the bishop is busy visiting hard-hit communities in what he calls a "consolation tour," to promote forgiveness. He also spreads devotion to the Rosary, because he believes Jesus said it would help the people to heal and forgive. Bishop Dashe has a strong devotion to the Mother of God, whom he affectionately refers to as "Mamma Mary." He knows that she is with the people in their struggle against Boko Haram.

He also believes that one day his diocese will recover from the horror of these days, thanks to Mary's intercession. "These terrorists...think that by burning our churches, burning our structures, they will destroy Christianity. Never," the bishop said during the conference in Spain. "It may take a few months or a few years... but 'Boko Haram is gone.'"

He told EWTN News, "Prayer, particularly the prayer of the Rosary, is [what] will deliver us from the claws of this demon, the demon of terrorism. And of course, it is working."

Chapter Twelve

PRAYING THE ROSARY WELL

The Holy Rosary is the storehouse of countless blessings.[1]
—OUR LADY TO BLESSED ALAN DE LA ROCHE

The Rosary is a form of meditative prayer that can lead us to contemplation. As we meditate on the mysteries of our salvation presented to us through the events in the lives of Jesus and Mary, we are richly blessed, and so is the whole world. As we have said throughout this book, there seems to be a particular efficacy in praying the Rosary in this, our time.

Following then are some suggestions to help us pray the Rosary more effectively so we can reap the countless blessings it offers for us, our families, our Church, and our world.

COMMON OBJECTIONS TO THE PRAYER
OF THE ROSARY

When asked why a person doesn't pray the Rosary, three main objections are most typical: time constraints, distractions, and repetition.

No doubt about it, the Rosary takes time to pray. It may not take long to "say" or to "recite" the Rosary, but to *pray* it is another matter completely. That takes time, and our day does have to be arranged to accommodate it.

What about distractions? If you have prayed with any regularity for any length of time, you already know that distractions are a part of a life of prayer, no matter the form. And distractions don't necessarily lessen over time. Distraction is one of the three "plagues" of prayer. The other two are discouragement and dryness or aridity. In the case of the Rosary, because of its length, distractions can come regularly and persistently.

And then there is the encompassing repetitive nature of the Rosary—the same prayers over and over again, decade after seemingly never-ending decade. Some people find this repetition either so monotonous that they grow bored or so comforting that they are lulled to sleep.

But many saints attest to the efficacy of the Rosary. St. Francis de Sales tells us, "The greatest method of praying is to pray the Rosary," and St. Bernardine of Siena exhorts, "Recite your Rosary with faith, with humility, with confidence, and with perseverance."[2] Our Lady told Blessed Alan de la Roche that the angels rejoice and the Blessed Trinity delights when we pray the Rosary. She said, "After the Holy Sacrifice of the

Mass, there is nothing in the Church I love as much as the Rosary."[3]

The Rosary has the capacity to take us to new depths of prayer. It leads to a mystical experience of the mysteries of Christ's life and strengthens us in the truths of the faith. "Never will anyone who says his Rosary every day," said Our Lady, "become a formal heretic or be led astray by the devil."[4]

So do we fall victim to the difficulties we encounter as we pray the Rosary, or do we mount a defense against them? We must take the latter course of action, knowing that God will meet our meager generosity of heart with His boundless, generous love.

STRATEGIES FOR PRAYING THE ROSARY

Here are some strategies to help you pray the Rosary more effectively and to help you overcome the three difficulties of time constraints, distractions, and the lull of repetition.

Plan to pray the Rosary, and even *schedule* it if necessary. Resolve to pray the Rosary every day. And plan *when* to pray it—first thing in the morning, during your lunchtime, after dinner, before bed—and *where* to pray it—in church before the Blessed Sacrament, in a quiet place at home, at the park, on the train or in an airplane, in the car during your commute or in the pick-up line at your children's school. By planning your *when* and *where*, the Rosary will become part of your mind-set and part of your day.

Be prepared for distraction. Everyone, even the most spiritually advanced, experiences distraction in prayer. Distraction is one of the tactics the Evil One uses to tempt us away from prayer altogether. We ought not to be surprised. The *Catechism of the Catholic Church* calls prayer a battle (see *CCC*, 2725–2745).

A variety of aids can help us maintain our attention and a prayerful disposition of heart. These effective "weapons" include Rosary meditation CDs, Sacred Scripture, holy literature, and religious music. These can help us remain attentive so we can mine the treasures of grace waiting for us in each decade.

Place yourself in the presence of the Blessed Mother and the Holy Spirit before you pray, and ask for their guidance. It is always spiritually prudent to entrust ourselves to the "holy duet" of the Blessed Virgin Mary and the Holy Spirit as we begin to pray. This is especially so as we prepare to pray the Rosary. Our Blessed Mother and the Holy Spirit can assist us in entering into the mysteries of Christ. One lovely prayer is simply this: "Come, Holy Spirit, come by means of the powerful intercession of the Immaculate Heart of Mary, your well-beloved spouse."

Change your speech pattern as you pray the Rosary. We can all "get lost" as we pray a long prayer, our minds drifting far from the discipline at hand. To help maintain a prayerful attitude of heart while praying the Rosary, try changing your speech pattern.

1. You can *alter the cadence* you are using. Slow down, pausing to consider the words you are saying and the mystery they are revealing. Linger a while to reflect on, enter into, or beg God to take you more deeply into

the mystery at hand. Ask Him to imbue the innermost confines of your heart with the mystery you are praying. At other times, speed up the cadence, not to "get through" the Rosary but to express the spiritual delight of it.

2. *Move from praying the Rosary silently to praying it out loud or vice versa*—especially if you have drifted off or are getting lulled by the prayer. If you pray the Rosary out loud, *change the tone* you use throughout the recitation—softer, louder, less emphasis on a word, more emphasis—especially in light of the mystery being prayed. Allow the sentiments of your heart to move you from meditation to contemplation to thanksgiving, to praise, back to meditation, back to contemplation. The Holy Spirit will take you along the continuum and pray through you.

Announce each mystery, suggests Pope St. John Paul II in *Rosarium Virginis Mariae* (*RVM*, 29). He also suggests using an icon of the mystery to help focus our attention. This can stimulate our imagination and lead us more deeply into the sacred truth the mystery expresses. If you do not have an icon, a holy picture or statue can substitute.

Pause at the name of Jesus. This is another practical suggestion from Pope St. John Paul II. He tells us that the name of Jesus is the "center of gravity" in the Hail Mary and the "hinge" that joins its two parts. A too hasty recitation of the prayer can overlook this center of gravity and cause us to lose connection with the mystery we are contemplating.

Insert a clause with the name of Jesus to highlight the mystery being contemplated. This is a long-standing custom in many places, to help fix attention on the mystery being prayed.

- The same clause could be repeated for all ten Hail Marys. For the first sorrowful mystery, for example: "*And blessed is the fruit of thy womb, Jesus, as He travailed in the Garden of Gethsemane.*

- Or a different clause could be inserted with each Hail Mary, to "tell the story" of the mystery: "And blessed is the fruit of thy womb, Jesus, as He entered the garden with the apostles." "And blessed is the fruit of thy womb, Jesus, as He saw the disciples asleep." "And blessed is the fruit of thy womb, Jesus, as the blood rained from his pores," and so on. This suggestion by Pope Paul VI is both beautiful and helpful.[5]

Direct the prayers to the Persons of the Blessed Trinity, one by one, or to Mary, perhaps under her different titles. Pray as if each is there with you, for indeed, each is. Pause and ask questions of Mary, of Jesus, of God the Father, and of the Holy Spirit:

- For example, with the first joyful mystery: "Mother, what was it like when you were fecundated by the Holy Spirit? As I continue to pray this Hail Mary, mystically take me into that moment in your life, and give me at least some taste of it."

- Or after one of the Our Fathers: "Father God, your Son tells us that you give us our daily bread. What 'bread' do I most need today? Is it the bread of consolation, of charity, of long-suffering? Help me to eat of this bread, that I might be more like your Son."

This type of dialogue illustrates St. Teresa of Avila's definition of prayer as "nothing else than...taking time to be alone with him who we know loves us" (CCC, 2709).

St. Bernardine of Siena, too, tells us something quite lovely:

> You must know that when you "hail" Mary, she immediately greets you! Don't think that she is one of those rude women of whom there are so many—on the contrary, she is utterly courteous and pleasant. If you greet her, she will answer right away and converse with you!"[6]

Offer your prayer of the Rosary in reparation for sin or as intercession for the needs of others and the world. The Rosary is a powerful prayer of intercession and petition. Recall that Our Lady at Fatima asked the children to pray the Rosary every day for peace in the world. We can pray an entire Rosary in intercession for one particular need, or we can pray it for a variety of intentions. When praying for a specific person, inserting the intercession or petition in the second half of the Hail Mary can be quite effective in keeping our focus: "Holy Mary, Mother of God, pray for John now and at the hour of his death, Amen." "Holy Mary, Mother of God, pray for the healing of those who are addicts, now and at the hour of their death, Amen."

The Rosary is a powerful weapon to help us face our personal trials and tribulations as well as the ones we face corporately. In the unprecedented challenges we face today, we need to pick up these holy beads with confidence and regularity. We hope these tips and practical insights will help you make use of this great prayer that heaven has given us.

HOW TO PRAY THE ROSARY

If you have never prayed the Rosary before, or haven't prayed it for a long time, here you will find both instructions to guide you as well as the prayers of the Rosary. May these inspire your journey toward the grace God has for you to receive and to share!

1. Holding the crucifix, pray the Sign of the Cross:

   In the name of the Father and of the Son and of the Holy Spirit. Amen.

2. Then profess the Apostles' Creed:

   I believe in God, the Father Almighty, Creator of heaven and earth; and in Jesus Christ, His only Son, Our Lord; who was conceived by the Holy Spirit, born of the Virgin Mary, suffered under Pontius Pilate, was crucified, died, and was buried. He descended into hell; the third day He arose again from the dead. He ascended into heaven and sits at the right hand of God, the Father Almighty; from thence He shall come to judge the living and the dead. I believe in the Holy Spirit, the Holy Catholic Church, the communion of saints, the forgiveness of sins, the resurrection of the body, and life everlasting. Amen.

3. On the first medal or bead, pray the Our Father:

   Our Father, who art in heaven, hallowed be thy name.

Thy kingdom come, thy will be done, on Earth as it is in heaven. Give us this day our daily bread, and forgive us our trespasses, as we forgive those who trespass against us. And lead us not into temptation, but deliver us from evil. Amen.

Note: If you are praying with a Warrior's Rosary, you may wish to seek the intercession of the saint whose image is on the Our Father medal. This can come at the end of the meditation by simply saying, "St. _____, pray for me (us)."

4. On the next three beads, pray the Hail Mary, one per bead, asking for an increase in the virtues of faith, hope, and love:
    Hail Mary, full of grace, the Lord is with thee. Blessed art thou among women, and blessed is the fruit of thy womb, Jesus. Holy Mary, Mother of God, pray for us sinners, now and at the hour of our death. Amen.

5. Next, pray the Glory Be:
    Glory be to the Father, and to the Son, and to the Holy Spirit. As it was in the beginning, is now, and ever shall be, world without end. Amen.

6. Option: If desired, add the Fatima Prayer, requested by Our Lady at Fatima: O my Jesus, forgive us our sins, save us from the fires of hell, lead all souls to heaven, especially those in most need of thy mercy.[7]

7. At the beginning of each decade (set of ten beads) is an Our Father medal or bead. Announce the mystery to be contemplated. Pause and reflect on this mystery, perhaps

by using the Warrior Rosary meditations in chapter eleven. Then pray the Our Father.

8. Pray a Hail Mary on each of the next ten beads, keeping in mind the mystery you are contemplating.

9. Each decade concludes with the Glory Be and the Fatima Prayer.

10. Repeat steps 7–9 for all subsequent decades. After completing all five mysteries (decades), conclude with the Hail, Holy Queen:

Hail, holy Queen, Mother of Mercy, our life, our sweetness, and our hope. To thee do we cry, poor banished children of Eve. To thee do we send up our sighs, mourning and weeping in this valley of tears. Turn then, most gracious advocate, thine eyes of mercy toward us, and after this our exile, show unto us the blessed fruit of thy womb, Jesus. O clement, O loving, O sweet Virgin Mary.

V. Pray for us, O Holy Mother of God

R. That we may be made worthy of the promises of Christ.

11. Some choose to add the following:

V. Let us pray,

R. O God, whose only Begotten Son, by His life, death, and resurrection, has purchased for us the rewards of eternal life, grant, we beseech thee, that while meditating on these mysteries of the most holy Rosary of the Blessed Virgin Mary, we may both imitate what they contain and obtain what they promise, through Christ our Lord. Amen.

V. May the divine assistance remain with us.

R. And may the souls of the faithful departed rest in peace. Amen.

Most Sacred Heart of Jesus, have mercy on us.

Immaculate Heart of Mary, pray for us.

When the Rosary is said in a group, or individually before the Blessed Sacrament, a plenary indulgence may be obtained by praying one Our Father, one Hail Mary, and one Glory Be for the intentions of the Holy Father.

12. Prayer to St. Michael: St. Michael the Archangel, defend us in battle. Be our protection against the wickedness and snares of the devil. May God rebuke him, we humbly pray, and do thou, O Prince of the heavenly hosts, by the divine power, thrust into hell Satan and all the evil spirits who prowl about the world seeking the ruin of souls. Amen. End with the Sign of the Cross. This can be done while holding the Rosary's crucifix.

IN CONCLUSION

Clearly, at this moment in the history of man, the Rosary belongs in the hands of every man, woman, and child. God has chosen us for this time and this time for us. Everything about our day and age—all of our personal struggles and difficulties as well as the challenges we face in the world—God uses as instruments to lead us to purification and sanctification. And perfected by Him through the crucible of trial, we become conduits of the saving power of Christ. In faith, let us ask for the strength, the grace, and the wisdom to engage the spiritual battle using heaven's weapon of choice—the Rosary!

We come to the close of this book with one more testimony, and it could not be a more appropriate one. God is speaking to us today in abundant ways. May we pay heed!

A Rosary Story

The Rosary of Intercession

Vinny Flynn

Most of us who pray the Rosary usually offer it for some specific intention, often multiple intentions, relating to our own needs or the needs of others. Typically, the intention is stated or mentally acknowledged at the beginning of the Rosary, and then more or less forgotten or relegated to the back of our mind as the prayers themselves are recited. Has this ever happened to you?

I would like to suggest a way that the Rosary can easily be adapted to incorporate our specific intention so that we remain conscious of it and reoffer it throughout the prayers and meditations. By remaining conscious of the intention while we pray and meditate on the mysteries, we link the person we are praying for (ourselves or someone else) to the persons of Christ and Mary *in a very meaningful and active way*. Doing this helps us discern more completely the specific needs of the person for whom we are praying, and our single, general intention continually reemerges in a series of specific intentions. Prayed in this way, the Rosary can become a very complete and effective prayer of discernment and intercession.

Pope John Paul II was so fond of saying the Rosary is a Gospel prayer. *We are remembering and pondering with Mary the great mysteries of God's love.* We are there, reliving the story of our salvation, and thus our prayer is, in a very real sense a living prayer. Through our intentions, we can bring others with us, lifting them up into these living mysteries and *repeatedly asking for God's loving, healing action in their lives.*

So there is no set formula, but I can give you a few samples to get you started. At the beginning of the Rosary, offer the overall intention. Here are some examples, but don't be bound by them; use whatever words are most natural for you.

Thank you, Holy Spirit, for prompting me to pray for (name). Help me to know how to pray for (him/her/them), and as you guide my meditations, overshadow (him/her/them) with your healing love and let your intentions be fulfilled.

Or, if you have a more specific intention in mind:

Eternal Father, in Jesus's name, in union with your Holy Spirit, I offer you this Rosary through the intercession of the Immaculate Heart of Mary. Throughout these prayers and meditations, I lift (name) up to you, asking that you immerse (him/her/them) completely in your love. And I especially ask that... (here include your specific intention for that person or persons).

After the Apostles' Creed and the Our Father (which many people offer for the Holy Father), the first three Hail Mary's are usually offered for an increase in faith, hope, and love. These may easily be adapted to fit the particular person being prayed for:

Before the first Hail Mary: "Mary, intercede now for (name) for a deeper faith in God the Father."

Before the second Hail Mary: "Mary, intercede now for (name) for a greater hope and trust in Jesus."

Before the third Hail Mary: "Mary, intercede now for (name) for a fuller indwelling of love from the Holy Spirit."

Then, as you begin meditating on each mystery, try to mentally bring the person you are praying for into each event of that mystery. You can do this at the beginning of each mystery and continue it throughout your meditation. The more you do this, the easier it becomes. Some possible intentions for the Annunciation, for example:

"Mary, you were in prayer when the angel visited you. Your whole life had been consecrated to the Lord, and you were ready to hear His word. Intercede now for (name) to have that same devotion to prayer and readiness to hear the Lord.... Let (him/her/them) learn to be unafraid and to trust in the Lord with You, to say 'Yes' to Him with you and be ready to receive whatever the Lord chooses to give."

If you look for ways to apply the Gospel events and teachings of each mystery to the particular person you're praying for, you will find many different little prayers coming to mind that will keep the intention active and present to you as you pray. Mary is our great intercessor with the Lord, and interceding with her through the Rosary can be an especially uplifting and fruitful way to pray for those we love.

Vinny Flynn is a singer, writer, speaker, teacher, and counselor who uses his gifts and talents to help people understand the teachings of the Catholic Church and the devotion of the Divine Mercy. The author of numbers of books, including Seven Secrets of the Eucharist, *you can read more about him at www.vinnyflynn.com.*

Acknowledgments

When Servant approached me about writing a book on the Rosary, I saw it as a graced opportunity. If ever there was a time to evangelize the Rosary, that time is now! The project had long been in my heart, and I am most grateful for Servant's efforts in making it a reality. From the onset, I knew that I wanted my friend and colleague Thomas K. Sullivan to be part of the project. For years, we have discussed the Rosary as the necessary weapon to face the challenges of our time and the powers and principalities that incite them. We have "sharpened swords together" on this topic countless times. Along with his many insights, Tom's military experience and acumen brought a depth to the content that could not have been there otherwise.

In a special way, I want to thank my editor and friend, Heidi Hess Saxton. We have known each other since the mid-1990s and have walked through many moments together, both personally and professionally. As always, I am grateful for her good guidance and, most definitely, for her patience—something I am certain I tried over and over again!

And many thanks to Lucy Scholand, whose careful editing and excellent suggestions helped to make this book what Tom and I hoped it could be.

An additional thank-you to Michael Frazier for the cover design, and to Kelly McCracken, Kelly Hudson, and Katie

Carroll for their help and assistance in the last phase of completion.

A debt of gratitude to Susan Brinkmann, staff journalist of Women of Grace, whose contributions to the biographies of the saints were a huge blessing. Kudos to you, dear lady!

And thank you to Mike Aquilina, Diane Bates, Fr. Donald Calloway, David Calvillo, Dion DiMucci, Vinny Flynn, Scott Hahn, Fr. Wade Menezes, Donna-Marie Cooper O'Boyle, Heidi Hess Saxton, and Tom Sullivan for their candid testimonies about the priority of the Rosary in their lives. I am certain their stories and suggestions will inspire and encourage many souls.

A big thank-you to Jean Prather and Mary Dillenback (Regional Coordinator for *Women of Grace* in northern New York State), our "focus team," for their astute comments, insights, and suggestions on the manuscript. "Roses and honey" to you, sweet daughters of Our Lady!

Tom and I are very grateful to our families and friends for their prayers and their encouragement. Tom's beautiful wife, Carol Sullivan, has been a true *ezer* to both of us throughout the writing process. A thank-you to my family members who listened to me lament in the difficult moments and "high-fived" me in the joyful ones. Much gratitude, too, to my husband, Anthony, and my son, Simon. As St. Pope John XXIII tells us, our deceased loved ones are not separated from us but only invisible to us. They surely were fighting with us and for us during the writing process. *Hua*, guys!

Thank you also to the staff of *Women of Grace* and to the many *Women of Grace* members, facilitators, and regional coordinators who have prayed for us throughout these many months of writing and editing. You are gracious daughters of the Most High God and wonderful "sacred sisters."

Most importantly, thank you, dear Blessed Mother, for your intercession and maternal beatitude, which we certainly felt from the inspiration of this book to its completion. You have procured for us every grace we needed and helped us to cooperate with each. And thank you, Father God, Jesus Our Lord, and Holy Spirit, for all that you have done and for all that you will do for your people at this moment in history. May we receive the fullness of life that you intend for us!

Notes

Introduction

1. St. Dominic, as quoted in John M. Haffert, *Sign of Her Heart* (Washington, NJ: Ave Maria Institute, 1971), 218.

2. Our Lady of Fatima, as quoted in "The Revelation of the Two Hearts in Modern Times," https://www.ewtn.com/library/MARY/FIRSTSAT. HTM.

Chapter One

1. St. Padre Pio, as quoted in Fr. Stephano M. Manelli, *Padre Pio of Pietrelcina* (New Bedford, MA: Franciscans of the Immaculate, 1999), 88.

2. Pope Pius XII, *Ingruentium Malorum*, 15.

3. See Fulton J Sheen, *The World's First Love: Mary Mother of God* (San Francisco: Ignatius, 2010), 209.

4. In the first four centuries of the Church's history, it was the custom of the pagans to place crowns of roses on their statues as symbols of their devotion. The Christian faithful substituted prayers as signs of their love.

5. Rev. Math Josef Frings, *The Excellence of the Rosary: Conferences for Devotions in Honor of the Blessed Virgin* (New York: Aeterna, 1912), 6.

6. Rev. Bernard O'Reilly, LD, *True Men as We Need Them: A Book of Instruction for the Men in the World* (New York: P.J. Kenedy, 1878), 216. The fifty repetitions of the *Ave* were also known as the Psalter of the Incarnation or of the Blessed Virgin.

7. O'Reilly, 217.

8. Exorcists today continue to attest to the Rosary's power in freeing souls from demonic influence.

9. Fr. Johann Roten, SM, "Rosary Origins," International Marian Research Institute, University of Dayton, https://udayton.edu/imri/mary/r/rosary-origins.php.

10. A two-year-long revolt of Muslims, *Moriscoes*, in Granada, located in Spain's Andalusia region.

11. Brandon Rogers, commentary in G.K. Chesterton, *Lepanto: With Explanatory Notes and Commentary,* ed. Dale Ahlquist (San Francisco: Ignatius, 2004), 60.

12. Chesterton, 62, quoting the *Atlantic Monthly*, December 1857, 139.

13. Along with the defeat of the Turks came the end of oared galleys. Henceforth, sails and broadside cannons would determine military outcomes.

14. Christopher Check, "The Battle That Saved the Christian West," *Catholic Answers Magazine*, vol. 18, no. 3 (March 2007), http://www.catholic.com/magazine/articles/the-battle-that-saved-the-christian-west.

15. Congregation for the Doctrine of the Faith, "The Message of Fatima," http://www.vatican.va/roman_curia/congregations/cfaith/documents/rc_con_cfaith_doc_20000626_message-fatima_en.html.

16. See Becky Yeh, "The Abortion Ripple Effect: Russia's Tragic Abortion Tale," June 27, 2014, liveactionnews.org; Christopher Read, *The Collapse of Tsarism and the Establishment of Soviet Power* (Hampshire, U.K.: Palgrave MacMillan, 2013), 136.

17. This section on Fatima is adapted from my Women of Grace Foundational Study Guide: *Full of Grace: Women and the Abundant Life* and Young Women of Grace Study Guide: *Embrace Your Femininity*, both published by Simon Peter Press.

18. "Aurora Borealis Startles Europe," *New York Times*, late city edition, January 26, 1938, 25.

19. The exact number of casualties is unknown for a variety of reasons, including inaccurate census reports. Some estimates put the number at approximately two hundred thousand, though others say this number is overly conservative.

20. Hubert F. Schiffer, *The Rosary of Hiroshima* (Washington, NJ: Blue Army of Our Lady of Fatima, 1953), 10.

21 Atomic Heritage Foundation, "Bombings of Hiroshima and Nagasaki—1945," http://www.atomicheritage.org/history/bombings-hiroshima-and-nagasaki-1945.

22. See "Hiroshima and Nagasaki Death Toll, Children of the Atomic Bomb: A UCLA Physician's Eyewitness Report and Call to Save the World's Children," https://prezi.com/6pehgr_eeuuu/the-decision-to-drop-the-atomic-bomb/.

23. Schiffer, 10.

24. On March 25, 1984, "Pope John Paul II, 'united with all the pastors of the Church in a particular bond whereby we constitute a body and a college,' consecrates 'the whole world, especially the peoples for which by reason of their situation you have particular love and solicitude.' Both the pope and Sr. Lucia initially seemed uncertain that the consecration has been fulfilled, but shortly thereafter Sr. Lucia tells the papal nuncio to Portugal that the Consecration is fulfilled." "Fatima Consecration: Chronology," EWTN, https://www.ewtn.com/expert/answers/FatimaConsecration.htm.

25. "Our Blessed Lady and the 20th Century," *The Flock*, vol. 17, no. 2 (Summer, 2013), 15.

26. Clarence W. Hall, "The Country That Saved Itself," *Reader's Digest*, November 1964, 133.

27. Dr. Glycon de Paiva, one of the counterrevolutionaries, is quoted by Clarence W. Hall in "The Country That Saved Itself": "It's the classic communist tactic to give the impression that they [the agitators] are many. Actually, only a dedicated few are needed to accomplish the downfall of a country. Free peoples make the error of discounting any force not present in huge numbers. We learned that lesson the hard way." Hall, 6.

28. Hall, 3–4.

29. Hall, 9.

30. Hall, 14.

31. Hall, 9.

32. Hall, 9.

33. See "Famous Rosary Miracles," Miraculous Rosary blog, miraculous-Rosary.blogspot.com.

34. Pope Benedict XVI, "Letter Concerning the Remission of the Excommunication of the Four Bishops Consecrated by Archbishop Lefebvre," March 10, 2009, https://w2.vatican.va/content/benedict-xvi/en/letters/2009/documents/hf_ben-xvi_let_20090310_remissione-scomunica.html.

CHAPTER TWO

1. "The Final Report of the 1985 Extraordinary Synod of Bishops," pt. 2, A, no. 4, EWTN, https://www.ewtn.com/library/CURIA/SYNFINAL.HTM.

2. Karol Wojtyla, as quoted in Frank Reniewicz, *For God, Country, and Polonia: One Hundred Years of Orchard Lake School* (Orchard Lake, MI: Center for Polish Studies, 1985), 146.

3. Cardinal Karol Wojtyla, Bicentennial Talk, as quoted in Fr. C. John McCloskey III, "The Final Confrontation," The Catholic Thing, June 1, 2014, https://www.thecatholicthing.org/2014/06/01/the-final-confrontation/.

4. *Christifidelis Laici*, 14; see Romans 8:18.

5. John Paul II, "Address to the Symposium of the Council of European Bishops' Conference," October 11, 1985, 13.

6. Pope John Paul II at Castel Gandolfo, August 26, 1996, quoted in "Pope John Paul II's Teaching on the Martyrs of Our Century," http://www.vatican.va/jubilee_2000/magazine/documents/ju_mag_01031997_p-56_en.html.

7. See Pope John Paul II, "Apostolic Letter for the Fourth Centenary of the Union of Brest," November 12, 1995, https://w2.vatican.va/content/john-paul-ii/en/apost_letters/1995/documents/hf_jp-ii_apl_19951112_iv-cent-union-brest.html.

8. Pope John Paul II, *Tertio Millennio Adveniente*, 37.

9. Pope John Paul II, "Bull of Indication of the Great Jubilee of the Year 2000," 13.

10. Pope John Paul II, Address at 15th World Youth Day Vigil of Prayer, (Tor Vergata, August 19, 2000), 4, http://w2.vatican.va/content/john-paul-ii/en/speeches/2000/jul-sep/documents/hf_jp-ii_spe_20000819_gmg-veglia.html.

11. Pope John Paul II, "Homily of the Holy Father John Paul II" (17th World Youth Day, July 28, 2002), 2, 3, 5. https://w2.vatican.va/content/john-paul-ii/en/homilies/2002/documents/hf_jp-ii_hom_20020728_xvii-wyd.html.

12. See "Beatifications during Pope John Paul II's Pontificate," http://www.usccb.org/about/leadership/holy-see/john-paul-ii/beatifications-during-pope-john-paul-iis-pontificate.cfm.

13. According to Catholic spirituality and teaching, redemptive suffering is the belief that all our sufferings can be united to the Passion of Jesus to great spiritual benefit for ourselves and for others. It is what St. Paul talks about in Colossians 1:24. Our sufferings are opportunities to enter into the salvific action of Jesus Christ through which redemptive grace flows.

14. Cardinal Stanislaw Dziwisz, "A Life with Karol," as quoted in "John Paul II's Secretary: Pontificate Was Marked by Martyrdom," Catholic News Agency, Krakow, April 11, 2014, http://www.catholicnewsagency.com/news/john-paul-iis-secretary-pontificate-was-marked-by-martyrdom/.

15. Dziwisz, "A Life with Karol."

16. Rev. John Trigilio, Jr., PhD, ThD, Rev. Kenneth Brighenti, PhD, Rev. Johnathan Toborowsky, MA, *John Paul II for Dummies,* special edition (Hoboken, NJ: John Wiley & Sons, 2006), 86.

17. George Weigel, *Witness to Hope: The Biography of Pope John Paul II* (New York: Harper Perennial, 2001), 57.

18. John Paul II, "Address to the Participants in the 8th Mariological Colloquium," October 13, 2000, 1, available at https://www.saint-mike.org/library/papal_library/john_paulii/addresses/october_13_2000.html.

19. Pope John Paul II, quoted in Stefano De Fiores et al., *Jesus Living in Mary: Handbook of the Spirituality of St. Louis Marie de Montfort* (Bay Shore, NY: Montfort, 1994), 1225.

20. Pope John Paul II, "Letter of John Paul II to the Montfort Religious Family," 1.

CHAPTER THREE

1. Office of the Chairman, the Joint Chiefs of Staff, *Department of Defense Dictionary of Military and Associated Terms* (Washington, DC: U.S. Government Printing Office, 1994), 158.

2. See Decree on the Apostolate of the Lay People, 2.

3. Pope Pius XI, as quoted in Sam Guzman, "A Powerful Weapon: 15 Quotes on the Holy Rosary," The Catholic Gentleman, http://www.catholicgentleman.net/2014/10/powerful-weapon-15-quotes-holy-rosary/.

4. See Sun Tzu, *The Art of War* (Wichita, KS: WaterMark, 2010), 20.

5. See Karol Wojtyla, *Love and Responsibility* (San Francisco: Ignatius, 1993), 96–97.

6. See St. Thomas Aquinas, *Summa Theologiae,* 108:4, in "Angels: From the Teachings of Saint Thomas Aquinas," Catholic Spiritual Direction, http://www.jesus-passion.com/angels.htm.

7. Msgr. Paul J. Glenn, *A Tour of the Summa* (St. Louis: Herder, 1960), 47–48.

8. *Catholic Encyclopedia*, s.v. "Angels," http://www.newadvent.org/cathen/01476d.htm.

9. Fr. H.M. Manteau-Bonamy, OP, *Immaculate Conception and the Holy Spirit* (Libertyville, IL: Marytown, 2008), 77.

10. Manteau-Bonamy, 78.

11. Fr. Pascale Parente, *The Angels in Catholic Teaching and Tradition* (Charlotte, N.C.: TAN, 2013), 58–59.

12. Manteau-Bonamy, 78.

CHAPTER FOUR

1. A dear priest friend once shared that he and a rabbi met regularly for study of the Bible. In studying Genesis, the rabbi remarked that one school of rabbinic scholarship maintains that the breezy time of the day (Genesis 3:8) is about 3:00 PM. When the priest shared with him that 3:00 PM was the time of Jesus's death on the cross, the rabbi was stunned. For the priest, this pointed to the reality that Jesus Christ is indeed the New Adam. Isn't God good!

2. Harold Burke-Sivers, *Behold the Man: A Catholic Vision of Male Spirituality* (San Francisco: Ignatius, 2015), 19.

3. See Pope John Paul II, *Theology of the Body: Human Love in the Divine Plan* (Boston: Pauline, 1997), 35–37.

4. John Paul II, *Theology of the Body*, 57.

5. John Paul II, *Theology of the Body*, 60.

6. Burke-Sivers, 20–21.

7. Matthew Henry, as quoted in Herbert Lockyer, *All the Women in the Bible* (Grand Rapids, MI: Zondervan, 1967), 13.

8. For more about the authority of woman, read Dr. Monica Miller's *The Authority of Women in the Catholic Church* (Steubenville, Ohio: Emmaus Road, 2015).

CHAPTER FIVE

1. St. Irenaeus, *Against Heresies*, bk. III, chap. 22, no. 4, http://www.newadvent.org/fathers/0103322.htm.

2. All Scripture passages in this book come from the *Revised Standard Version Catholic Edition* unless otherwise noted. This translation does not indicate that Adam was with Eve at the time of her temptation.

3. Maximilian Kolbe, *The Writings of St. Maximilian Maria Kolbe*, Volume II, Various Writings, General Editor, Antonella Di Piazza, FKMI (Lugano, Italy: Nerbini International, 2016), 2281- 2281.)

4. Gertrud von le Fort, *The Eternal Woman* (San Francisco: Ignatius, 2010), 3.

5. Von le Fort, 3.

6. Von le Fort, 4.

7. A philosopher himself, Pope John Paul II speaks of such things regarding woman in his theology of the body and in his writings specific to women, such as *Mulieris Dignitatem* and *Letter to Women*, as well as portions of *Familiaris Consortio* and *Evangelium Vitae*.

8. See Exodus 26:31–33; 36:35–26; 40:13, 21; 1 Kings 8:6–9; Leviticus 16:2; Hebrews 9:3–4; 6:19–20; 9:11–12; 10:19–22; Matthew 27:51; Luke 23:44–46.

9. The word *inspire*, to fill someone with the urge or ability to do something, comes from the Latin *inspirare*, which means to "blow into or breathe upon." The root of *inspirare* is the Latin *spirare*, which means "to breathe," the noun of which is *breath*. The word *breath* has always been connected with life. Genesis 2:7 illustrates this: "Then the Lord God formed man of dust from the ground and breathed into his nostrils the breath of life; and man became a living being." Interestingly, the noun *inspiration* has as one of its definitions "the immediate influence of God or a god," which would refer to *grace*.

10. See "To Women," from the Closing Messages of the Second Vatican Council, December 8, 1965; Monica Migliorino Miller, *Sexuality and Authority in the Catholic Church* (Scranton, PA: University of Scranton Press, 2007), xi.

11. Man references God as First Cause in yet another way: Every egg in a woman's body develops when she is still in the womb, at around fourteen weeks of gestation. When she comes of age, an ovary will release one egg a month. The egg's fertilization by the male sperm brings forth a new human person. It is the sperm that initiates the life. Man, therefore, images God as First Cause in that, in the natural order, his action initiates life.

12. Note that the serpent was a dragon as opposed to a snake. If it had been simply a snake, the penalty of crawling on its belly would make no sense, since that is what it would have been doing. But a dragon has legs. Therefore, through this penalty, God cut the very legs out from under the Evil One.

13. *Lumen Gentium*, 62.

14. St. Louis de Montfort, *True Devotion to Mary* (Rockford, IL: TAN, 1985), 28.

15. Quoting *Lumen Gentium*, 62.

16. De Montfort, *True Devotion*, 24.

17. The latter days began with the passion, death, and resurrection of Jesus Christ. Church documents, mystical phenomena in the way of apparitions and locutions, as well as the *sensus fidelium* suggest that we are approaching the eschatological moment of Revelation 12.

18. De Montfort, *True Devotion*, 50.

19. De Montfort, *True Devotion*, 54.

Chapter Six

1. Pope Leo XIII, as quoted by Father Emil Neubert, *Queen of Militants* (St. Meinrad, IN: St. Meinrad's Abbey, 1947), 101.

2. Fr. Neubert, SM, was born in 1878 in Ribeauville, France. He did much to win souls for Christ by promoting devotion to Our Blessed Lady. He made his academic mark in a thesis called "Mary in the Pre-Nicene Church," the first patristic thesis dedicated to Mary. Fr. Neubert was the author of many spiritual classics on Our Lady.

3. Neubert, 98.

4. Neubert, 98.

5. In this same paragraph, the Holy Father reminds the faithful that Pope John XXIII urged the prayer of the Rosary to invoke the "great grace" of the Spirit of God for the Church before convening the Second Vatican Council, which opened in 1962, forty years prior to the promulgation of this Letter. This is not an incidental comment. Perhaps, once again through the prophetic gaze that so marked him and his pontificate, John Paul II knew that the Rosary was going to be of special efficacy in the years to come, through the power of the Holy Spirit, in a type of quasi-annunciation of the people of God.

6. The *Catechism* cites St. Ignatius of Loyola, *Spiritual Exercises*, 104.

7. Paragraph 10 of *Rosarium Virginis Mariae* seems to contain the fruit of the Holy Father's own contemplation. It has the feel of a "gaze" into his own heart and relationship with Our Lady, as he meditates most likely on the Joyful Mysteries. Deeply touching and very fatherly.

8. Peter Toon, "Remember, Remembrance," http://www.biblestudy-tools.com/dictionaries/bakers-evangelical-dictionary/remember-remembrance.html.

9. See Fr. William Wagner, ORC, "Sacramentals: Means of Grace and Help," *Opus Sanctorum Angelorum*, Summer 1994, available at www.opusangelorum.org.

10. To see the development of the pope's theology on this, read the entire section 15 in *Rosarium Virginis Mariae*.

11. Dr. Anthony L. Lilles, *Fire from Above: Christian Contemplation and Mystical Wisdom* (Manchester, NH: Sophia Institute, 2016), 172.

12. See also *RVM*, 15. Here the saint provides us with more insight about Mary's role in conforming us to Christ. Speaking of his motto, *Totus Tuus*, he quotes St. Louis de Montfort from his *Treatise on True Devotion to Mary*: "The motto is of course inspired by the teaching of Saint Louis Marie Grignon de Montfort, who explained in the following words Mary's role in the process of our configuration to Christ: '*Our entire perfection consists in being conformed, united and consecrated to Jesus Christ*. Hence the most perfect of all devotions is undoubtedly that which conforms, unites and consecrates us most perfectly to Jesus Christ. Now, since Mary is of all creatures the one most conformed to Jesus Christ, it follows that among all devotions that which most consecrates and conforms a soul to our Lord is devotion to Mary, His Holy Mother, and that the more a soul is consecrated to her the more will it be consecrated to Jesus Christ.'"

13. De Montfort, *True Devotion*, 33.

14. De Montfort, *True Devotion*, 35.

15. De Montfort, *True Devotion*, 36.

16. For a lovely meditation on this concept, see Father Gabriel of St. Mary Magdalene, OCD, *Divine Intimacy* (Oil City, PA: Baronius, 2014), 233.

17. For a beautiful narrative on the transforming effect of Christ's dialogue with the woman at the well, read the chapter, Strategy 2, "Engage in Prayer," in Johnnette Benkovic, *Experience Grace in Abundance: Ten Strategies for Your Spiritual Life* (Manchester, NH: Sophia Institute, 2015).

18. Lilles, 174–175.

19. Benkovic, *Experience Grace in Abundance*, 275–276.

20. De Montfort, *True Devotion*, 47, 48, 59.

CHAPTER SEVEN

1. Ignatius Loyola as quoted by Susan Tassone in *Day by Day for the Holy Souls in Purgatory: Daily Reflections* (Huntington, IN: Our Sunday Visitor, 2014), entry for January 15.

2. Jerry Boykin and Stu Weber, *The Warrior Soul: Five Powerful Principles to Make You a Stronger Man of God* (Lake Mary, FL: Charisma, 2015), 143.

3. Litany of St. Joseph, http://ewtn.com/Devotionals/Litanies/joseph.htm.

4. Some theologians consider this moment to be Joseph's annunciation. See Fr. Marie-Dominque Phillippe, OP, *The Mystery of Joseph*, (Bethesda, MD: Zacchaeus, 2010), 13.

5. Phillippe, *The Mystery of Joseph*, 15–16.

6. Paul Thigpen, *Saints Who Battled Satan: Seventeen Holy Warriors Who Can Teach You How to Fight the Good Fight and Vanquish Your Ancient Enemy* (Charlotte, NC: TAN, 2015), 16.

7. The titles for the saints come from the Pater Noster medals on the Warrior's Rosary designed by Thomas K. Sullivan.

8. See *Catholic Encyclopedia*, s.v. "St. Michael the Archangel," newadvent.org.

9. Excerpt from Edmund Spenser, *The Faery Queen*, as quoted in *Cyclopedia of English Literature: A Selection of the Choicest productions*, ed. Robert Chambers (Boston: Gould, Kendall and Lincoln, 1847), vol. 1, 89.

10. Mary Purcell, *The First Jesuit* (Westminster, MD: Newman, 1957), 22–23,

11. Paul Thigpen, *Manual for Spiritual Warfare* (Charlotte, NC: TAN, 2014), 189.

12. Fr. Paolo Pirlo, SHMI (1997), "St. Louis," in *My First Book of Saints* (Manila, Philippines: Sons of Holy Mary Immaculate, Quality Catholic Publications, 2014), 193–194.

13. St. Louis, "From a Spiritual Testament to His Son," second reading in the Office of Readings for the Feast of St. Louis, July 13, http://www.liturgies.net/saints/louis/readings.htm.

14. Francis de Sales in *Treatise on the Devout Life*, as quoted in "Saint Francis de Sales, Bishop, Doctor of the Church—1567–1622," http://www.ewtn.com/library/MARY/DESALES.htm.

15. Excerpt from *Lives of Saints* (New York: John J. Crawley, 1954) quoted in "Saint Francis de Sales, Bishop, Doctor of the Church—1567–1622" at ewtn.com.

16. "Saint Isidore of Seville," CatholicSaints.Info, http://catholicsaints.info/saint-isidore-of-seville/.

17. Charles F. Montalembert, *Les Moines d'Occident depuis Saint Benoît jusqu'à Saint Bernard* [*The Monks of the West from Saint Benedict to Saint Bernard* (Paris: J. Lecoffre, 1860), as quoted in "St. Isidore of Seville," Catholic Online, http://www.catholic.org/saints/saint.php?saint_id=58.

18. St. Isidore of Seville, as quoted in Ronda Chervin, *Quotable Saints* (Oak Lawn, IL: CMJ Marian, 1992), 55.

19. Braulio, *Elogium* of Isidore, appended to Isidore's *De Viris Illustribus.*

CHAPTER EIGHT

1. Francis Johnston, *The Wonder of Guadalupe: The Origin and Cult of the Miraculous Image of the Blessed Virgin in Mexico* (Rockford, IL; TAN, 1981), 12.

2. "Our Lady of Guadalupe," Catholic Online, http://www.catholic.org/about/guadalupe.php.

3. "Our Lady of Guadalupe," Catholic Online, http://www.catholic.org/about/guadalupe.php.

4. "Our Lady of Guadalupe." Juan would later learn that Our Lady had appeared to his uncle upon his deathbed, and had healed him. He described her as being young and surrounded by a soft light as she gently told him, "Call me and my image Santa Maria de Guadalupe."

5. Thigpen, *Saints Who Battled Satan*, 26–27.

6. Thérèse of Lisieux, "The Night of the Soul," from *Story of a Soul*, http://www.storyofasoul.com.

7. Thérèse of Lisieux, "Letter to Father Belliere," in *Lettres de Sainte Thérese de l'Enfant-Jésus* (N.p.: Office Central de Lisieux, 1948).

8. Thérèse of Lisieux, *The Story of a Soul*, study edition, trans. John Clark, OCD (Washington, DC: Institute for Carmelite Studies, 2005), 299–300, emphasis in original.

9. Thérèse of Lisieux, Letter (no. 89) Celine, April 26, 1889; Letter to Leonie, May 20, 1894, *Correspondance Générale* (Paris: Éditions du Cerf-Desclée de Brouwer, 1972).

10. Summarium of the Process of Beatification and Canonization 1, testimony of Celine, 2753.

11. Pope John Paul II, "Proclamation of St. Therese of the Child Jesus and the Holy Face as a 'Doctor of the Church.'" https://w2.vatican.

va/content/john-paul-ii/en/homilies/1997/documents/hf_jp-ii_
hom_19101997.html.

12. Michael Joseph Cerrone III, *For God and Country: The Heroic Life and Martyrdom of St. Joan of Arc* (Manchester, NH: Sophia Institute, 2015), 35.

13. The dauphin is the eldest son of the king of France. Charles VII was not technically the eldest, but his four brothers had died.

14. Etienne Robo, *The Holiness of Saint Joan of Arc* (London: Incorporated Catholic Truth Society), reprinted courtesy of Eternal Word Television Network, https://www.ewtn.com/library/MARY/JOAN1.HTM.

15. Robo.

16. Robo.

17. Robo.

18. Robo.

19. Clare of Assisi, "The Testament of Saint Clare," http://www.liturgies.net/saints/clare/testament.htm.

20. Sarah Gallick, *The Big Book of Women Saints* (San Francisco; Harper, 2007), 240.

21. Gallick, 349.

22. St. Clare of Assisi, quoted in Melissa Musick, "Memorial of St. Clare of Assisi," The Catholic Catalogue, http://thecatholiccatalogue.com/tag/st-clare-of-assisi/.

23. "Saracen, in the Middle Ages, [was] any person—Arab, Turk, or other—who professed the religion of Islam," *Encyclopedia Britannica*, s.v. "Saracen," https://www.britannica.com/topic/Saracen.

24. Tomasso da Celano, *The History of Saint Clare, Virgin*, quoted in "Eucharistic Miracle of Saint Clare of Assisi," http://www.therealpresence.org/eucharst/mir/english_pdf/Assisi.pdf.

CHAPTER NINE

1. De Montfort, *True Devotion*, 26–27.

2. De Montfort, *True Devotion*, 33–34.

3. Pope Benedict XVI, "Letter to the Bishops of the Catholic Church Concerning the Remission of the Excommunication of the Four Bishops Consecrated by Archbishop Lefebvre," March 10, 2009, https://w2.vatican.va/content/benedict-xvi/en/letters/2009/documents/hf_ben-xvi_let_20090310_remissione-scomunica.html.

4. See Ann Ball, *Young Faces of Holiness: Modern Saints in Photos and Words* (Huntington, Ind.: Our Sunday Visitor, 2004), 188–192.

5. St. José Sánchez del Río, as quoted in "José Anacleto González Flores and Eight Companions," http://www.vatican.va/news_services/liturgy/saints/ns_lit_doc_20051120_anacleto-gonzalez_en.html..

6. St. Maximilian Kolbe, as quoted in Patricia Treece, *A Man for Others: Maximilian Kolbe, Saint of Auschwtiz, in the Words of Those Who Knew Him* (New York: Harper & Row, 1982), 134–135, and cited in Robert

Royal, *The Catholic Martyrs of the Twentieth Century: A Comprehensive World History* (New York: Crossroad, 2000), 210.
7.   Antonio Ricciardi, OFM Conv., *St. Maximilian Kolbe: Apostle of Our Difficult Age* (Boston: Daughters of St. Paul, 1982), 45–56, cited in Royal, 202.
8.   Royal, 202.
9.   André Frossard, *N'Oubliez pas l'amour: La Passion de Maximilien Kolbe* (Paris: Editions Robert Laffont, 1987), cited in Royal, 203.
10. Royal, 207.
11. Royal, 210.
12. Bruno Borgowiec, quoted in "St. Maximilian Kolbe, Priest Hero of a Death Camp," catholic-pages.com.
13. Homily of Pope John Paul II, Beatification of Fr. Jakob Kern, Sr. Restituta Kafka and Fr. Anton Maria Schwart, Sunday, June 21, 1998, 7, https://w2.vatican.va/content/john-paul-ii/en/homilies/1998/documents/hf_jp-ii_hom_19980621_austria-beatification.html.
14. UCAN Spirituality, "Blessed Maria Restituta," http://spirituality.ucanews.com/2013/10/29/blessed-maria-restituta/.
15. Royal, 135.
16. "Blessed Maria Restituta."
17. "Blessed Maria Restituta."
18. Homily of Pope John Paul II.
19. Venerable Faustino, as quoted in Ball, 63–64.
20. Venerable Faustino, as quoted in Ball, 66.

CHAPTER TEN
1.   De Montfort, *True Devotion*, 28.
2.   Reniewicz, 146.
3.   It is interesting to note that the destruction of religion and the family were the top two priorities of the Russian social revolution. In 1917, abortion became legal there, as did divorce for any reason. In 1973, three years before Wojtyla's address at Orchard Lake Schools in Michigan, the right to abortion and no-fault divorce became law in the United States of America, following the lead of European countries. Also of interest is the fact that Sr. Lucia wrote in a letter that Our Lady, who had appeared to her more than one time following the Fatima apparitions, told her the final attack of Satan would be the attack against the family.
4.   Joseph Ratzinger, *Faith and the Future* (San Francisco: Ignatius, 2006), 92, emphasis added.
5.   Popularly attributed to parliamentarian Edmund Burke.
6.   De Montfort, *True Devotion*, 35–36.
7.   *St. Michael and the Angels: A Month with St. Michael and the Holy Angels* (Charlotte, NC: TAN, 2008), 118.
8.   Fr. Henri Marie Boudon, as quoted in *St. Michael and the Angels,* 118.
9.   De Montfort, *True Devotion*, 28.

10. St. Bonaventure, as quoted in Thigpen, *Manual for Spiritual Warfare*, 124.

11. St. Louis de Montfort, as quoted in Thigpen, *Manual for Spiritual Warfare*, 123.

12. De Montfort, *True Devotion*, 54.

13. De Montfort, *True Devotion*, 54, 59.

14. For more information, go to http://www.themostholyRosary.com/indulgences.htm.

15. Pope St. Melchiades (AD 311–314), as quoted in "The Sacrament of Confirmation," My Catholic Source, http://www.mycatholicsource.com/mcs/pc/sacraments/confirmation.htm.

16. For more information on the Warrior's Rosary and to obtain one, visit shop.womenofgrace.com. And whether you have one of these unique Rosaries or not, we hope the following meditations inspire your prayer.

CHAPTER ELEVEN

1. Quoted in John Paul Thomas, *Daily Reflections for Ordinary Time: Weeks 18-34* (N.p.: My Catholic Life, 2016).

2. See "The Battle of Prayer," *CCC*, 2725–2745.

CHAPTER TWELVE

1. Our Lady to Blessed Alan de la Roche, as quoted in Francis W. Johnston, *The Voice of the Saints: Counsels from the Saints to Bring Comfort and Guidance in Daily Living* (Charlotte, NC: TAN, 1965), chap. 6.

2. St. Bernardine Siena, as quoted by Raphael Brown in *Saints Who Saw Mary* (Charlotte, NC: TAN, 1955), 34.

3. Our Lady to Blessed Alan de Roche, as quoted in St. Louis de Montfort, *The Secret of the Rosary* (Bay Shore, NY: Montfort, 1969), 120.

4. De Montfort, *Secret of the Rosary*, 62.

5. See Pope Paul VI, "Apostolic Exhortation for the Right Ordering and Development of Devotion to the Blessed Virgin Mary," *Marialis Cultus*, 46, February 2, 1974, https://w2.vatican.va/content/paul-vi/en/apost_exhortations/documents/hf_p-vi_exh_19740202_marialis-cultus.html.

6. Brown, *Saints Who Saw Mary*, 36.

7. In an interview with author William Thomas Walsh, Sr. Lucia stated, "The correct form is the one I have written in my account of the apparition of July 13: 'O my Jesus, pardon us, and save us from the fire of hell; draw all souls to heaven, especially those most in need.'" This version does not have the commonly added phrase "of thy mercy" at the end of it. See William Thomas Walsh, *Our Lady of Fátima* (New York: Image, 1990), 220.